Geometry and the Silversmith
The Domcha Collection

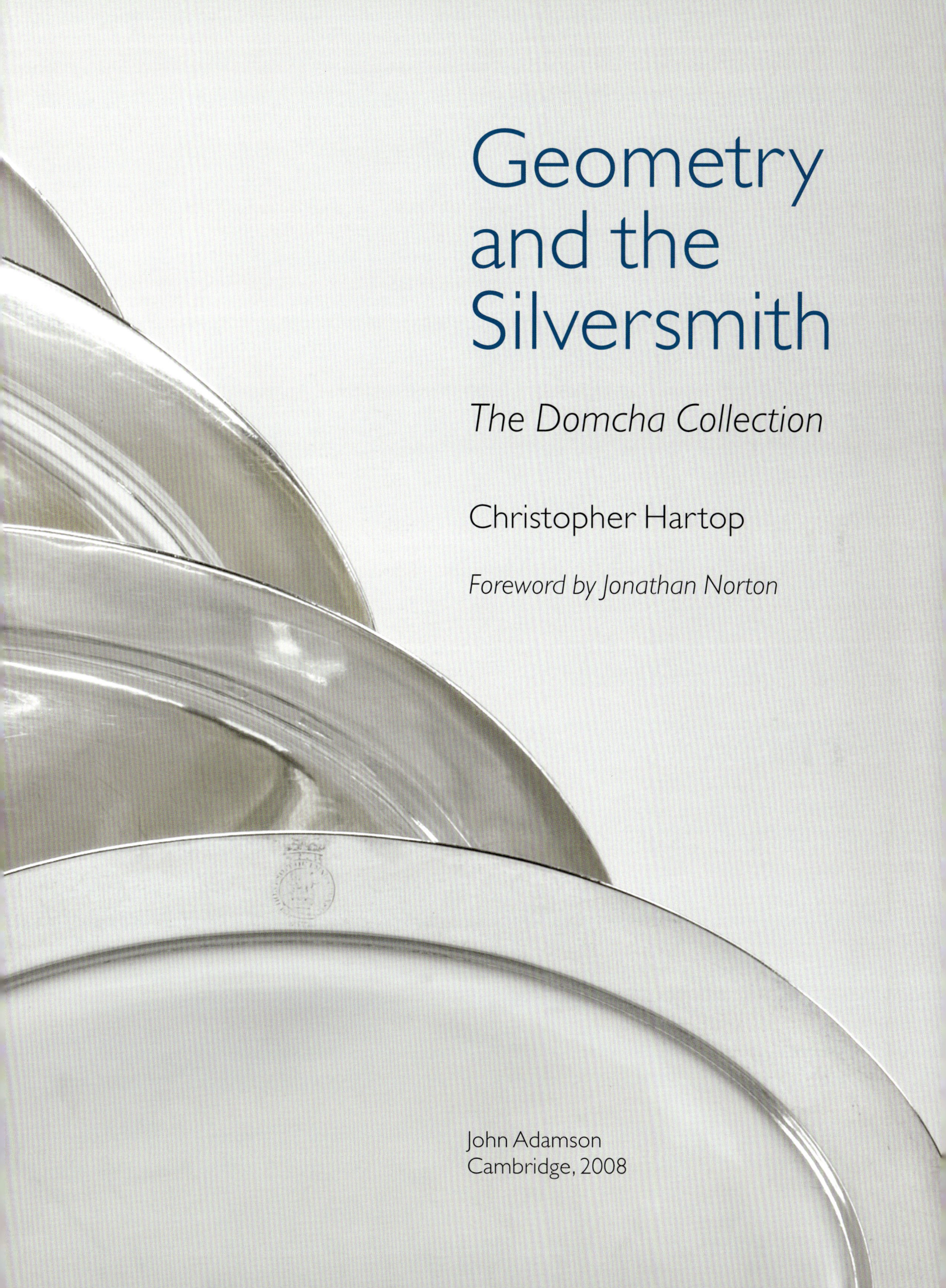

Geometry and the Silversmith

The Domcha Collection

Christopher Hartop

Foreword by Jonathan Norton

John Adamson
Cambridge, 2008

By the same author

The Huguenot Legacy: English Silver 1680–1760
1996

East Anglian Silver 1550–1750 (editor)
2004

Royal Goldsmiths: The Art of Rundell & Bridge 1797–1843
2005

A Noble Feast
2007

British and Irish Silver in the Fogg Art Museum, Harvard University
2007

John Adamson,
90 Hertford Street, Cambridge CB4 3AQ, England

Copyright © John Adamson, 2008
Text © Christopher Hartop, 2008
Photographs of objects © The Domcha Collection, 2008

Photographs unless otherwise credited were taken by Amanda Harvey and Rick Jenkins of Sotheby's.

The right of Christopher Hartop to be identified as the author of this work has been asserted by him in accordance with the Copyright, Designs and Patents Act, 1988.

First published 2008

All rights reserved. No part of this publication may be reproduced or transmitted in any form or by any means, electronic or mechanical, including photocopy, recording or any other information storage and retrieval system, without prior permission in writing from the publisher or a licence permitting restricted copying. In the United Kingdom such licences are issued by the Copyright Licensing Agency, 90 Tottenham Court Road, London W1T 4LP.

British Library Cataloguing in Publication Data

A catalogue record for this book is available from the British Library.

ISBN: 978-0-9524322-8-9

Set in Gill Sans Light and designed by James Shurmer

Printed on Burgo Larius 150 gsm matt by Conti Tipocolor, Italy

Contents

Foreword	*page* 7
Acknowledgements	8
Geometry and the silversmith	9
The catalogue	23
About the catalogue	24
Glossary	118
Bibliography	121
Picture credits	124
Index	124

Unknown English artist, *The Tea Party* (c. 1725). Oil on canvas. *Courtesy of the Worshipful Company of Goldsmiths, London*

Foreword

Building up relationships with collectors and watching their collections grow are among the most rewarding aspects of antique dealing. With the Domcha Collection, we have had the pleasure of assisting a family over five generations in acquiring and refining collections in a number of fields. With this silver collection, strong lines and plain surfaces, where the colour and patina of the metal come beautifully to the fore, have always been dominant themes, so well exemplified in the magnificent octagonal coffee pot of 1728/29 engraved with the royal arms. But over the years some rather more ornate pieces have been acquired, such as the animal-head stirrup cups and the Punch and Judy condiment set, which provide an entertaining contrast to the geometric forms. In recent years, examples from outside Great Britain have been added to show how pervasive the taste for plain silver, with an emphasis on line rather than ornament, has been in continental Europe.

Sharing in the thrill of the chase in acquiring examples to add to this collection has also been pleasurable. We are delighted now to be guided by Christopher Hartop through the silver collection in its entirety as he meticulously explores its themes in this splendid catalogue.

Jonathan Norton
S.J. Phillips Ltd.

Acknowledgements

I am indebted to everyone at S.J. Phillips Ltd. in London for their help, especially Francis Norton, Jonathan Norton and Nicholas Norton. Roger Barton and his team were cheerful and efficient in the face of the many requests I made to them. Sotheby's generously provided the facilities for the photography, which was undertaken by Amanda Harvey and Rick Jenkins. Thanks are also due to Cynthia Harris and her colleagues in the silver department there, including Alice Bleuzen, Harry Charteris, John Culme and Claire Grindey. I am also grateful to Heath Cooper, Alexander Kader, Carolyn Miner, Liz Mitchell and Johanna Ward.

I also owe a special word of thanks to David Beasley, Jane Bradley, Tim Martin, Jet Pijzel-Dommisse, Matthew Stuart-Lyon and Gareth Willliams for their advice. Above all, I am grateful to Thomas Sinsteden for his insights into Irish silver, and to Peter Adamson of the University of St Andrews for his help with the complex world of geometry. It has been a pleasure to work again with James Shurmer, the book's designer, and with the team at Conti Tipocolor in Florence, the book's printers and binders. John Adamson has once again been a source of good advice as well as painstaking editing, and I am grateful to him for another fruitful and pleasurable collaboration. My wife Juliet has been my mainstay and right arm.

All catalogues stand on the shoulders of those that have gone before, and it is the often unsung work of dealers and auctioneers in researching objects they have handled that has been the backbone of much of the information in this catalogue. It is to them, past and present, that this book is dedicated.

Geometry and the Silversmith

> The world harmoniously confus'd,
> Where order in variety we see,
> And where, tho' all things differ,
> All agree.
>
> *Alexander Pope*

The importance of geometry

Geometry and working in precious metal have always been inextricably linked. At the most rudimentary level, the ability to scribe concentric circles using a compass on a sheet of silver is necessary to provide guidelines for the hammering which will raise it up into a bowl. The most simple, early, forms in silver were, like pottery, probably created without any preliminary design but shaped freely by the craftsman's hands into the simplest of vessels. But it was not long before a preconceived design, one with satisfying proportions that existed, as it were, outside the hands that held it, became usual. Greek and Roman silversmiths could create basic shapes using geometry, but it was in the Middle East and in East Asia that highly advanced geometric constructions were being used for metalwork. Only in recent years has this early silverwork been revealed, for example with the excavation of tombs in China, although many of the complex forms had long been known to scholars in the West through ceramic imitations of the succeeding centuries. Lobed geometric forms used for Sassanian silver wine cups of the seventh century AD travelled

Fig. 1 Detail of the frontispiece to William Robinson's *Proportional Architecture*, 1733. *Private collection*

with the Arabs to the Iberian peninsula, where they continued to be used for footed cups (*bernegales*) into the seventeenth century.[1]

To reproduce these deceptively simple looking forms, which utilize straight and curved lines, it was not merely a matter of copying. It required a certain level of understanding of geometry, and the ability to carry out geometric constructions. But most books on the history of silver making are curiously silent on the subject of geometry. Indeed the whole process of how designs have been transmitted to the workbench down the ages, through drawings, templates, models or in other ways, is a sadly unexplored part of European and American silver studies. Most works on the history of silver are divided into sections concerning the supply of the raw material, the manufacturing processes, the structure and regulation of the industry, and the design and ornament of surviving objects. But how were the designs formulated and disseminated? The problem, certainly before the middle of the eighteenth century, lies in what Timothy Schroder has called "evidence without documents"[2] – we have only the surviving objects to study, but very few documents. The notebook of Villard de Honnecourt, a mason working in France in the thirteenth century, is a tantalizing window on this creative world. It has two pages which include decorative geometric constructions and illustrations of simple solutions such as how to measure the circumference of a circle. But no similar manuscript appears to survive from a medieval goldsmith. The "mystery" of geometric drawing was probably as closely guarded by goldsmiths as it was by masons and this no doubt led to the deliberate destruction of many drawings and templates.[3]

It might be useful at this stage to define what one means when one speaks of geometry in the context of working in gold or silver. Every time a worker hammers a piece of metal, changing the plane, forming a shape, or creating angles or curves, he is, perhaps

Fig. 2 Zerubbabel having an ephod made of gold rings, from an English illuminated manuscript, c. 1340. A designer works on a geometric drawing while the goldsmith hammers on an anvil. *British Library*

unwittingly, using geometry, for geometry investigates the properties and relations of surfaces, lines and solids. Insofar as the term geometry has appeared in books on silver, it has usually been used, adjectivally, to describe either angular or plain silver. In both these areas, the presence of geometry in design and making is perhaps more clearly seen than in more ornate objects, but in this instance the term geometry is taken narrowly to refer to a style rather than a science. The so-called "geometric style" in English silver occurs during the first half of the eighteenth century. Both angular silver and the plain style will be addressed later, but first we should examine the place of the science of geometry in the creative and manufacturing processes of metalworking.

The exalted status of the goldsmith in Europe in the Middle Ages meant that a study of mathematics and Euclidean geometry was an essential part of their training, and early depictions of the goldsmith often show dividers among the tools on his bench. Knowledge of how to draw a polygon, a multifoil and an epicycloid was needed by a goldsmith as well as a mason. The trefoil, quatrefoil, hexafoil and octofoil, essential elements of Gothic architecture, all figure in medieval silver (figs. 3 and 4). Subtle geometric curves also played a part. The deceptively simple fig-shaped bowls of many late-medieval spoons are derived from mathematical curves such as the loops formed within a prolate cycloid,[4] and, it

Fig. 3 Octofoil in the tracery of a window in Amiens Cathedral, early fourteenth century.

Fig. 4 Octofoil in a silver paten, middle of the thirteenth century, belonging to the church of Wyke, Winchester, Hampshire.
Courtesy of the Worshipful Company of Goldsmiths, London

can be argued, are of a subtlety comparable to the curves of the crossing arches of Wells Cathedral.

In the Renaissance, geometry was used to explore the depiction of space in art. Paolo Uccello's drawing in the Uffizi uses geometry to understand the structure of the shapes forming a chalice, and to depict it accurately (fig. 5). Albrecht Dürer, the son of a goldsmith, used geometry to attempt to codify what today we call aesthetics. Indeed, goldsmiths were at the forefront of much of this new scholarship in aesthetics and perspective. Wenzel Jamnitzer's book of polyhedra, *Perspectiva Corporum regularium* of 1568, broke new ground in the study of perspective and the depiction of multifaceted solids. But most importantly for the working goldsmith, it was the categorization and publishing of myriad geometric shapes during the sixteenth and seventeenth century that offered him a wealth of models, and the knowledge to exploit them. The new educated patron, versed in the classical authors including Euclid, was probably as familiar with the science of design as the goldsmith himself. With the dramatic increase of surviving silver in England from the seventeenth century onwards, it becomes possible, when studying the Domcha Collection, to explore design conventions and to try to grasp the processes behind them.

One of the greatest attractions of objects made in England in the seventeenth and eighteenth centuries is their sense of harmony. Whether plain or exuberantly decorated, they have a balance and scale that makes them not only attractive but comfortable to

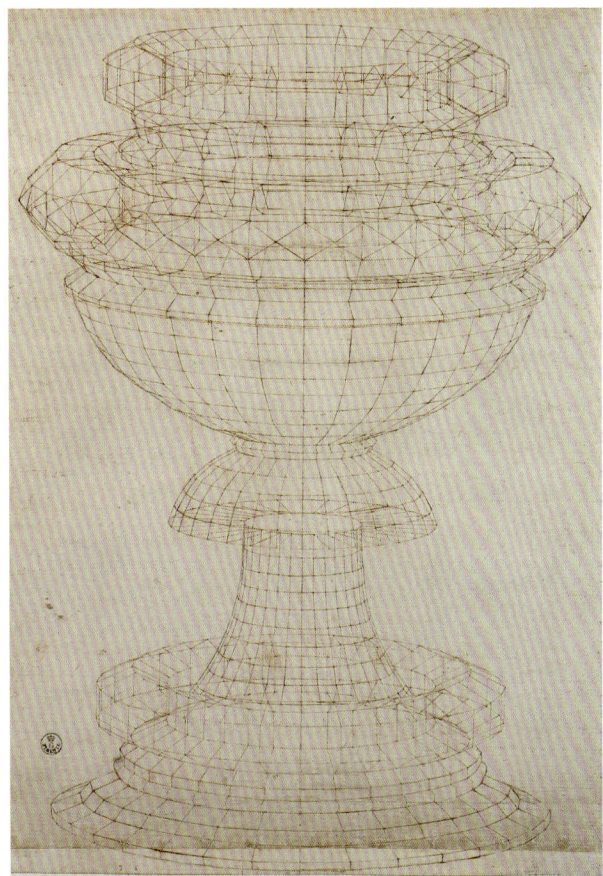

Fig. 5 Paolo Uccello, Drawing of a chalice, c.1450. *Gabinetto dei Disegni e delle Stampe, Uffizi Gallery, Florence/Scala*
Uccello uses geometry to analyze the design in depicting a chalice.

use.[5] It is not surprising that during the past hundred years silver made during this period, especially the plainer wares, has enjoyed pride of place among collectors of English silver. In fact so much plain silver survives from this period that in the twentieth century it was dubbed, misleadingly, an age of simplicity in design.[6]

The attraction of simplicity

It is easy to understand why in history this plain style has always been popular. Objects which rely on line rather than surface ornament have been made since ancient times, often existing alongside pieces with embossed ornament.[7] Rather than the intricacies of complex chasing, the smooth reflective surfaces of silver are a source of endless fascination, and the warm patina acquired with age adds to the appeal of antique pieces. It is geometry of planes and solids wrought in silver. As Carl Hernmark observed: "In themselves, simplicity of form and an undecorated surface can signify an object of little pretension, made perhaps by some goldsmith of but slight skill … Where we do become interested is when simplicity of form and a plain surface are used for aesthetic effect".[8] Its geometry, however, can be deceptively simple. The Swedish art historian Helena Dahlbäck Lutteman sounds a note of warning: "… a rich design, a vociferous appearance may impress and beguile simply with its abundance … A single line or a simple form needs to be perfect".[9]

Fig. 6 Polygonal silver porringer, London, 1655/56, mark WH mullet above, pellet in annulet below. *Fogg Art Museum, Harvard University Art Museums*
Both austerely plain linear silver and polygonal sections have been a theme in European silver from the early Middle Ages onwards. Polygonal-bodied vessels such as this one enjoyed a vogue in England in the middle years of the seventeenth century.

The aesthetic possibilities of plain reflective surfaces for objects which were more than merely utilitarian were constantly being explored. The stark simplicity of the fluted ewer and basin made by Jan Lutma for Amsterdam Council in 1655/56 had nothing to do with cost saving. At the same time in England porringers were being made with vertical fluting of stunning simplicity. This had not only the practical advantage of making the body more durable, but also making the most use of candlelight (fig. 6). Moreover, for personal use, simple forms have always been the most practical as it is much easier to keep smooth surfaces clean. This is particularly so for drinking vessels, and food containers such as salts.

The triumph of the polygon

It was in London from the 1680s to the 1730s that the polygon and other simple geometric shapes were widely and most successfully used by silversmiths. But to call it a "geometric style", as some writers of the last century did, is, as we have seen, a misnomer.

Of the polygons, the octagonal section was always the most popular shape. With its more obtuse interior angles it approaches a circle more closely than do pentagons and hexagons while retaining the aesthetically attractive angularity of its sides, and it has sufficient angles to give strength. It was used by medieval masons for the massive lantern on the transept of Ely Cathedral, and later by Brunelleschi for his dome in Florence. In silver, the square and the hexagon appear far less frequently than the octagon: it is easy to see how the sharp external angles of the square coffee pot by George Wickes in the Folgers Collection in the Cincinnati Museum could be susceptible to wear and damage (fig. 7). The hexagonal section, however, does not offer flat surfaces which enable one to apply a spout and handle at right angles to each other. Nonagonal cream jugs are known, and jugs with vertical multiple panelling enjoyed a brief vogue in the 1730s, but the importance of heraldic engraving in England during this period no doubt played a role in the popularity of the octagonal section for vessels as it provided a broad surface for a coat of arms or crest, which was often the only decoration on the piece.

Either a regular octagon or a square or oblong with canted corners was used for salts, dishes and candlesticks, but it was also popular for wares for coffee, tea and chocolate, either with straight or bowed outline.[10] The advent of these drinks in the middle of the seventeenth century demanded a variety of new vessels with which to serve them, and the tea table became a stage on which to display innovative fashionable wares – with a much more modest capital outlay than that required for the dinner service. But some of these seemingly simple shapes can be amazingly complex, such as the truncated octagonal pyramidal coffee pot, no. 53. Euclid does not discuss the ellipse, but other writers of classical times did. A fifth-century text gives instructions how to draw it, yet the form is almost non-existent in Gothic art. It was Kepler's work, *Ad Vitellionem Paralipomena*, published in 1604, that provided a practical means of drawing an ellipse using string and two pins and, from the early seventeenth century, the ellipse served as

Geometry and the Silversmith

a model for small silver saucers and dishes. Allowing for the inaccuracies of handwork, the modest spoon tray, no. 19, is an ellipse of stunning accuracy. The inventiveness with which the ellipse was used is noteworthy: the octofoil salver, no. 36, has lobes that may be considered as formed by the intersection of four ellipses with common centre. Aesthetically pleasing tension is created through the use of implied connection across the salver. On both the octagonal teapot, no. 44, and the hexagonal teapot, no. 50, any pair of opposite faces lies on the surface of a cylinder. In the case of no. 44, the cylinder is apparently elliptical whereas no. 50 shows a rather less determinate cross-section of cylinder.

By the end of the seventeenth century, the plethora of geometry books that had been published, mostly modelled on the works of Euclid, provided help in drawing the most intricate shapes with both straight and curved lines. For salvers, the guidelines could be scribed directly onto the prepared sheet of silver. Polygons could be drawn using a compass or pair of dividers and a straight-edge; "straight-edge and compass" methods can be used to construct five-, six-, eight-, ten-, twelve- and fifteen-sided polygons, but not seven-, nine-, thirteen- or fourteen-sided ones. Following the method devised by Euclid in his *Elements of Geometry*, a 15-gonal salver could be drawn using a succession of simple

Fig. 7 Silver coffee pot, London, 1745/46, mark of George Wickes. *The Folgers Collection, Cincinnati Art Museum*
The form of this pot, a truncated regular square pyramid, is virtually unique in English silver.
The acute angles make the body much more susceptible to damage and wear than the hexagonal and octagonal form.

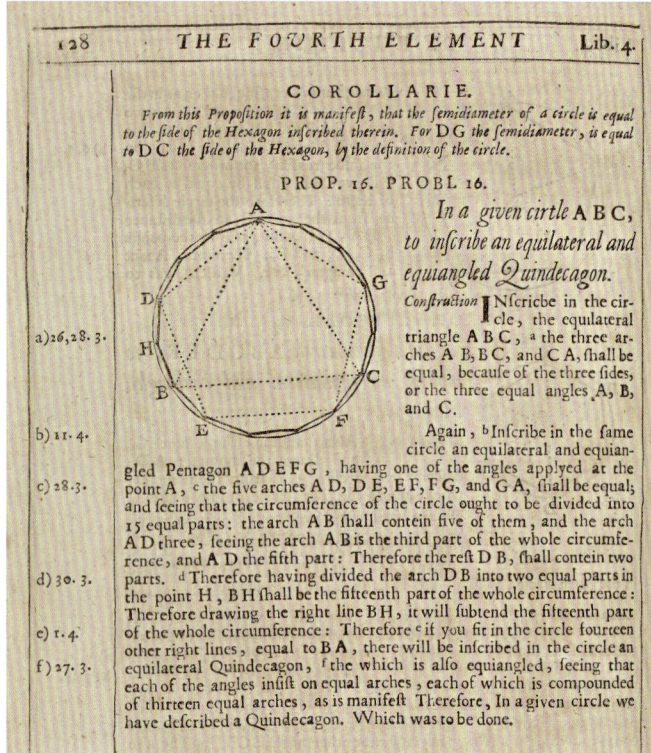

Fig. 8 Construction of a quindecagon, from Book 4 of Euclid's *Elements of Geometry published by the Care and Industry of John Leeke and George Serle, Students in the Mathematicks*, London, 1661. The Syndics of Cambridge University Library

Fig. 9 Fifteen-sided, or quindecagonal, silver-gilt salver, London, 1723/24, mark of Augustine Courtauld. *Christie's Images*

steps (figs. 8 and 9). Often these guidelines and centring marks are still to be seen on the backs of salvers. Euclid had first been translated into English in 1570 with a preface by John Dee. This preface has been described by E.G.R. Taylor, the eminent historian, as "a magnificent exposition of the relationship and application of mathematics, especially arithmetic and geometry, to the practice of various skilled arts and crafts".

Some early twentieth-century writers credited the Huguenots with the introduction of these shapes. However, geometric shapes in silver were, as we have seen, used long before the arrival in the 1680s of these religious refugees, and the marks of native English silversmiths are, if anything, more common on them. The first-generation Huguenots who are justly famous, such as Harache, Willaume and Platel, had large workshops which produced some simple wares, but for the most part their output was large-scale works in the international neo-classical baroque style that came by way of the Low Countries from France. This was aristocratic silver of dynamic surfaces with monumental fluting, bold vase shapes and heavy cast ornament which needed advanced technology and expertise. Hence production tended to be concentrated in the large workshops. In contrast, well-made geometric wares of the period are found with a multitude of makers' marks suggesting that a good deal of the production was outsourced to smaller workshops. Moreover, surviving French silver of the period shows that the straight line was much less popular there, and the polygon is much less prevalent.[11] Indeed polygonal silver is very much an English phenomenon, which in time spread to other European centres such as in the Low Countries and Hanover.

Although straight lines may be pleasing aesthetically, often our eye needs curves to soften the appearance of the things around us. Practically speaking, while we can enjoy the way angles between planes break the reflections into contrasting patches of light and shade, curved surfaces are better for the interiors of vessels designed to contain a beverage or food. The angles of the inside of the octagonal coffee pot, no. 53, are more difficult to keep clean than the curving base of the beer jug, no. 45. Moreover, curved surfaces can withstand wear and tear much more successfully, for the metal is then much more durable, and any dents and scratches are not so noticeable. We can still appreciate the play of light on convexes and concaves as well as the object's stark outlines.

For vessels, the combination of a polygonal cross-section with a serpentine outline became widespread at the end of the seventeenth century, and existed side by side with the straight sides of the truncated cone and pyramid. The baluster, when inverted, offered endless variety for candlesticks. Chinese porcelain ginger-jars were flooding the marketplace and provided the models for silver vessels. The bulging shoulder and flat base were experimented with for a time for casters and coffee pots, but soon it was recognized that for receptacles, for either liquid or dry substances, it was much more practical, for use and for cleaning, to have the bellied portion at the base of the object. The aesthetic attraction of the serpentine, and the baluster form, were analysed by William Hogarth in his *Analysis of Beauty*, published in 1753.

Proportion and harmony

For the educated patron in eighteenth-century England, the fine buildings and objects around them informed them with a sense of harmony and proportion. Hogarth argued that proportion was all-important: "The bulks and proportions of objects are govern'd by fitness and propriety. It is this that has established the size and proportion of chairs, tables, and all sorts of utensils and furniture," he wrote (fig. 10). When an eighteenth-century

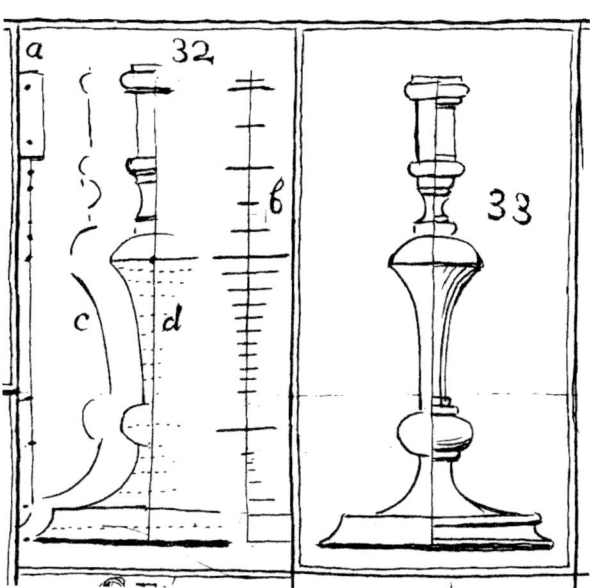

Fig. 10 Hogarth's attempts to analyse the proportions of the baluster and lobed sections of the stem of a candlestick, from plate 1 of *The Analysis of Beauty*, 1753.

The Domcha Collection

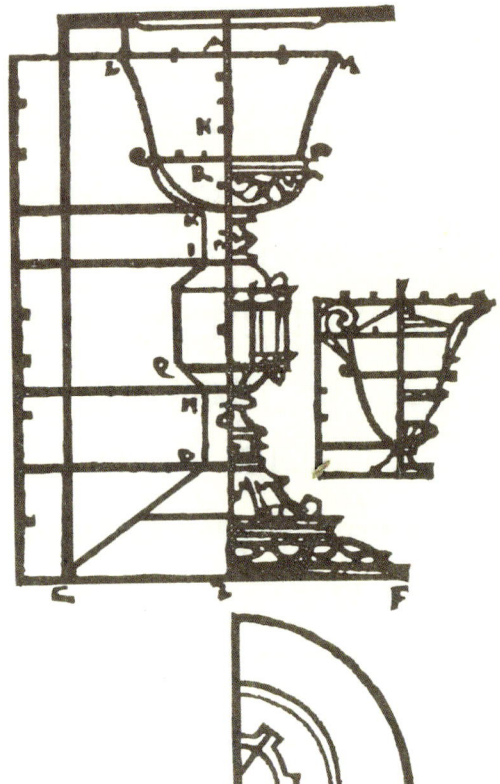

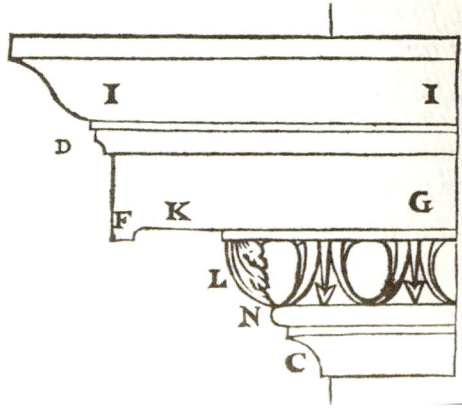

Fig. 12 (*above*) Architectural mouldings based on simple and complex geometric curves, plate from *Les Dix Livres d'Architecture de Vitruve, corrigez et tradvits nouvellement en François, avec des Notes & des Figures*, Paris, 1673, the first widely available edition of Vitruvius.
Similar mouldings were copied by London silversmiths for plain polygonal silver objects from the end of the seventeenth century onwards.

Fig. 11 (*left*) Juan de Arfe's drawings of a chalice and altar cruet showing the relative size of their components and their relative size to each other, plate from *De Varia Commensuración*.

goldsmith invoiced a "neat" cream jug, he and his patron understood that this meant well-proportioned and pleasing to the eye, in the same way as the five orders governed their architectural surroundings. In his book *De Varia Commensuración*, the sixteenth-century goldsmith Juan de Arfe, a Spaniard of Flemish ancestry, had sought to define correct proportions not only for the components of silver objects such as chalices and candlesticks, but also their size in relation to each other. Thus, an altar cruet was to be a third the height of a chalice (fig. 11). Symmetry was an essential element of this, but variations within certain closely defined parameters were also necessary. In silver, this can be seen in the contrast between straight lines and flat surfaces, and the baluster forms of spouts and ogee mouldings – a constant interplay of setting and releasing tension. Vitruvius's *De Architectura* (published in a French translation in 1686 and later, in the eighteenth century, in English) illustrated the variety of cyma curves in Greek and Roman architectural moulding which then began to appear on silverware (fig. 12), for example as mounts enclosing the reflective planes of the John Edwards coffee pot, no. 53. Other objects often have proportions that, if not the Golden Mean, are at least regular. For example, the dimensions of the Edwards coffee pot are based on a ratio of approximately 1:2. The height and the width from the outer edge of the handle to the tip of the spout form a square, and the sides are 2:1 to the diameter of the base. The tapering body of octagonal section is a truncated pyramid with a base that is half the height of the body.

Silver studies for much of the twentieth century were craftsman- rather than patron-orientated. When books assert that Queen Anne period silversmiths "preferred geometric shapes" it strikes a jarring note to us today, for we now acknowledge the customer's pivotal role in the adoption of new design during the period. This was something relatively new, for before the Renaissance the patron had not been expected, or permitted, to know the technical secrets of design. But in an age of educated patronage, Euclidean geometry was part of the education of a gentleman schooled in the works of the classical authors, and he would have been aware of the geometry of a plain object as much as the classical imagery of an ornate one. There is little doubt that a patron like William Duff, owner of at least two octofoil salvers (no. 36), would have been familiar with the way to draw an octofoil.

Use of the polygon and polyfoil in English silver waned in the 1730s and had all but disappeared by the middle of the century. But unadorned silver with an emphasis on line rather than ornamentation returned with the onset of neo-classicism in the 1760s. Now the emphasis was overwhelmingly on curved surfaces rather than the polygon, although polygonal shapes remained popular for inexpensive, machine-made tea wares such as those made in the Bateman factory at the end of the century. Moreover, totally unadorned silver lived on: the stark plainness of the Lord Bute's dinner service, no. 92, is a continuation of the tradition that was by then many centuries old.

The influence of Asia

We have seen that by the end of the seventeenth century there was a mass of published work showing how to draw complex geometric forms and that there is little doubt that educated patronage encouraged their use on silver. Yet it is most likely that the models for many of the forms were objects rather than diagrams in books. Most of these objects came from Asia, where an understanding of the science of geometry had developed at an early date and in some areas surpassed the writings of Euclid. Boat-shaped elliptical silver sweetmeat dishes or "sawcers" made in London in the 1620s copy ancient Chinese hardstone brush washers.[12] As we have seen, the use of the ellipse was something startlingly new in European decorative arts.

In the years following the Restoration, the Asian ceramics, lacquer and small quantities of metalwork being brought to England in rapidly increasing numbers provided inspiration for a host of new vessel forms. By far the largest category being imported was Chinese porcelain and stoneware. Porcelain had been known in England as a precious rarity since the Middle Ages but from the 1660s on it became a fashionable collectable. Then, as it became even cheaper, items filled London's shops, eventually becoming an everyday alternative to silver and pewter. Although the East India Company concentrated on tea and spices, their ship captains and officers were at liberty to transport their own cargoes of luxury goods. We have seen how the ginger-jar with bulging shoulder was adapted for coffee and chocolate pots. From the 1680s onwards, not only Chinese ceramics but also Kakiemon porcelain from Japan, often with delicately lobed or polygonal bodies, added to the variety of models available to the London silversmith.

The Domcha Collection

Fig. 13 Chinese silver wine pot, struck with hallmarks for London, 1682/83, mark TA. *Peabody Essex Museum, Salem, Massachusetts*
The body is a hexagonal oblate globe with six sides. Complex geometric forms such as these were taken up by London silversmiths. This is a rare example of a Chinese silver object known to have been in London in the 1680s, but the cheap Yixing stoneware copies of these expensive silver originals in a myriad of polygonal shapes were readily available to copy.

Perhaps the most important influence, however, lay in the Chinese geometrically shaped objects in red unglazed stoneware made in Yixing, and their imitations made by Johann Friedrich Böttger at Meissen and by John Dwight and others in England. A variety of examples appear, in company with London-made silver objects and mounted *exotica*, in the *vanitas* still lifes of the Dutch artist Pieter van Roestraeten, who worked in London in the second half of the seventeenth century. The pots were produced inexpensively, and were cut and polished like stone with technical brilliancy. Wine pots in the form of globes or cylinders panelled into four, six or eight sides were popular and were immediately copied in silver in London workshops. Ironically, this cheap stoneware was in reality copying expensive originals in precious metal. But the silver prototypes for these ceramic objects were seldom seen in London. One rare instance is a silver wine- or teapot which was assayed and hallmarked in London in 1682/83, probably in order for it to be offered for sale in a shop (fig. 13).[13] The shape of the pot is, like the London-made Simon Pantin teapot discussed above, a hexagonal oblate globe, but has a raised hexagonal collar. The same form was used by the Harache workshop for a silver-gilt kettle in 1695/96.[14] Asian lacquer also provided models for silver. Sets of square or oblong lacquer trays in graduated sizes, raised on bracket feet, were directly copied by London silversmiths (see no. 57). As with the red stoneware, the prototypes for the lacquer trays had been silver ones. Once again the design went from Asian silver to English silver by way of another medium.

The timelessness of the plain and the geometric

Interestingly, the exalted status which plain silver of the beginning of the eighteenth century acquired in the twentieth century bore no relation to its original cost. Workmanship, calculated on a per ounce basis in the eighteenth century, was generally charged at a lower rate for plain pieces than for ornate ones. Forming objects from sheets of silver required only small-scale casting for the moulded borders which held the piece together and gave it added durability. Apart from requiring more modest technology, making unadorned objects was a much more economical use of the material, for casting resulted in a heavier object. The shortage of silver in the late 1690s which resulted in the imposition of the higher Britannia standard for silverware, and the introduction of duty on wrought plate in 1720, both played a role. There are exceptions, however, and the royal coffee pot (no. 53), although plain, is as heavy as one with cast ornamentation. Here the unadorned and economical are exalted within this high-status object. This conceit is nothing new in precious metalwork: the 1632/33 tankard (no. 2), an inverted truncated cone, follows the form of the rough wooden tankards used since antiquity by the mass of the population, while the two pails in the Domcha Collection, one probably for ice (no. 93) and one a wine cooler (no. 99), remind one of Marie Antoinette's dairy at Rambouillet, furnished with milk pails (also truncated cones) made of Sèvres porcelain, a medium almost as expensive, and much more fragile, than silver. The clerk who entered the purchase of a similar silver wine cooler in Garrard's ledger in 1812 described it as "like a Common Pail" (see p. 110).[15]

Even in the nineteenth century unadorned silver was never entirely absent, and the popularity of plain silver in what became known as the "Queen Anne" taste spread rapidly at the beginning of the twentieth century.[16] Much was due to the influence of leading dealers such as S.J. Phillips and the late Commander G.E.P. How. How and his wife were united in their love of plain unadorned silver but indulged in a mock battle for the benefit of their customers in the pages of their *Silver Notes*, which were published annually in the 1940s. How was unwavering in his love of the octagon, while Mrs How preferred the gentle curves of the baluster shape. In 1946 How recollected: "Years ago, when bidding very high for a superb little George I octagonal piece, a Cockney voice on my left remarked 'Seems to be orl-right for them as 'as octagonal toiste', a statement which has left me with a warm feeling inside ever since".[17] Nevertheless, Mr and Mrs How were in complete agreement on the aesthetic mastery – and superb quality – of the Farren beer jug now in this collection, no. 45. As the commander said, writing about this object in 1947: "When plain silver is as fine as this it is indeed difficult to uphold one's defence of the decorated, but this is one of many exceptions which prove the rule, and the absolute tops in this plain silver of the Queen Anne–George I period does indeed take a very great deal of beating – *but it must be the tops*."[18] While not everyone would agree with How's dismissal of the ornate, his last sentiment strikes its own chord with all of us.

Notes

1. Such lobed wine cups were copied in China in the Tang dynasty, as the technique of raising silver by hammering replaced casting. A Sassanian silver-gilt example is in the Metropolitan Museum of Art, New York; for a Tang silver example of this form, see Masterpieces of Chinese Precious Metalwork, sale, Sotheby's, London, May 14, 2008, lot 51, and Jessica Rawson, "Chinese Silver and its Western Origins", *Connoisseur*, September, 1977, p. 37; for a Hispanic seventeenth-century example, see C. Esteras Martín, *La platería de la Colección Várez Fisa*, Madrid, 2000, p. 201, no. 78.

2. T. Schroder, "Evidence without documents: patterns of ornament in rococo and Régence silver", in V. Brett, ed., *Rococo silver in England and its colonies, Papers from a symposium at Virginia Museum of Fine Arts, Richmond, in 2004*, London, 2006, pp. 58–71.

3. John Harvey, *Medieval Craftsmen*, London, 1975, p. 88.

4. The path traced by a point on a fixed radius of a circle rolling on a straight line, where the point is outside the circumference of the circle. See Hartop, *Fogg*, p. 26.

5. Geometry and aesthetics go hand in hand, although from a careful study of the proportions of many of the objects in the Domcha Collection, it is evident that the Golden Ratio [φ] (approximately 1.618:1) was not used, at least consciously, by English silversmiths.

6. For a discussion of plain and ornate silver during the period, and the erroneous linking of plain silver to Protestantism, see Hartop, *Huguenot*, p. 65, and Hartop, "Patrons and Consumers".

7. The Jewel Office accounts in 1661 list "Gilt Plate some of it plain and some of it curiously chased & wrought".

8. Hernmark, vol. I, p. 59.

9. Helena Dahlbäck Lutteman, *The Triumph of Simplicity*, exh. cat., Nationalmuseum, Stockholm, 1988, p. 7.

10. In 1686 Horatio Townshend purchased "one Eight Square Salt" weighing 16 ounces from the goldsmith Richard Adams (Townshend Papers, Norfolk Record Office/MC1308/4/809X4). This was probably an octagonal "capstan" salt similar to one of 1676/77 belonging to the Skinners' Company and illustrated in Charles Oman, *Caroline Silver, 1625–1628*, London, 1970, plate 47B.

11. Polygonal cast candlesticks and dishes were, it is true, part of the standard repertory of the French silversmith at the beginning of the eighteenth century, but the attractions of the octagonal baluster in casters and other objects appear to have been confined to the north-east of the country, which can be explained by the military occupation of Lille by the English.

12. I am grateful to Jessie McNab for this suggestion.

13. H. Crosby Forbes, "Chinese Export Silver for the British Market 1660–1780" in *Transactions of the Oriental Ceramics Society*, vol. 63, 1998–99, pp. 1–18. Because of the hallmarks struck on it, the pot was long thought to be made in London but analysis of the alloy, as well as research into its manufacturing techniques, have convincingly shown it to be Chinese. The fact that it has an uninsulated silver handle, and the spout is positioned quite low on the body, suggest that it was intended for serving wine. Moreover, in China the hot water was poured directly onto the leaves in the cup making the use of a teapot unnecessary.

14. David Beevers, ed., *Chinese Whispers: Chinoiserie in Britain 1650–1930*, exh. cat., The Royal Pavilion & Museums, Brighton, 2008, p. 87, no. A12.

15. The idea lives on: a few years ago Tiffany & Co. produced silver baskets designed by Van Day Truex which copied the small wooden baskets, or punnets, that are used to sell strawberries in American supermarkets.

16. For twentieth-century attitudes to plain and ornate silver, and the implied moral superiority of plain silver, see Hartop, "Patrons and Consumers" and for the American taste for plain silver during the same period, see Alcorn, "Boston and the American Taste for British Silver" in Hartop, *Fogg*, pp. 17–22).

17. How, *Notes 1946–47*, p. 12.

18. How, *Notes, 1946–47*, p. 21.

The Catalogue

About the catalogue

In this catalogue the term "maker's mark" denotes the mark stamped on an object by the person who submitted it for assay at Goldsmiths' Hall in London, or at another assay office. This is not necessarily the same person as the one who made the object, and in fact most silver articles made during the period covered by this catalogue were the work of more than one individual. However, it has been decided to retain the term that has traditionally been used.

Specific dates of objects are provided by hallmarks, whenever present. In London, up to 1660, the date letter was usually changed in May each year; from 1660 to 1975 it was changed on May 29. Dates are therefore given thus: 1665/66. In other contexts, for example on documents, dates prior to 1752 are given in both Old Style (year beginning on March 25) and New Style (year beginning on January 1), thus: 1665–66.

The size of all objects is given in inches. The equivalent in centimetres (to one decimal place) is given in parentheses. Weights are given in troy ounces and pennyweights, the traditional way of weighing silverware. There are 20 pennyweights (dwt.) in a troy ounce (oz.), usually expressed in units of five. Where there is a wooden handle, such as on a coffee pot, a "gross weight" is given.

In England, the silver standard was sterling (925 parts per 1000) until 1697 when the legal (hallmarked) standard was raised to the Britannia standard (958/1000). In 1720 the sterling standard was resumed but the Britannia standard remained optional. In Ireland, the sterling standard has been used up to the present day, and the Britannia standard was never adopted. In Edinburgh, the legal standard was 916/1000 until at least 1759, after which Scotland adopted the sterling standard. With objects that have no hallmarks, the standard of the alloy can only be conjectured, hence the question mark before some of the specifications of standard.

The following abbreviations are used:
D. depth; *Diam.* diameter; *H.* height; *L.* length; *W.* width.

Provenance includes documented owners. A comma between the names of two owners indicates that the piece passed directly from the first to the second; a semi-colon indicates a gap in documentation. Without exception, all the objects in this collection were acquired from S.J. Phillips Ltd., London.

Abbreviations used in the Notes:

AAD: Archive of Art and Design, Victoria & Albert Museum, London

BL: British Library, London

NA [PRO]: National Archives (Public Record Office), Kew

Reference works cited under Maker's mark:

Bennett
Douglas Bennett, *Collecting Irish Silver*, London, 1984

Bowen and O'Brien
John R. Bowen and Conor O'Brien, *Cork Silver and Gold: Four Centuries of Craftsmanship*, exh. cat., Cork, 2005

Culme
John Culme, *The Directory of Gold & Silversmiths, Jewellers & Allied Traders, 1838–1914*, Woodbridge, 1987

Gill
Margaret A.V. Gill, *A Directory of Newcastle Goldsmiths*, Newcastle-upon-Tyne, 1980

Grimwade
Arthur G. Grimwade, *London Goldsmiths 1697–1837, Their Marks and Lives*, rev. edn., London, 1990

Hare
Susan Hare (ed.), *Paul de Lamerie: The Work of England's Master Silversmith*, exh. cat., Goldsmiths' Hall, London, 1990

Helft
Jacques Helft, *Le Poinçon des provinces françaises*, Paris, 1985

Jackson, 1921
Sir Charles Jackson, *English Goldsmiths and Their Marks*, London, 1921

Jackson
Ian Pickford (ed.), *Jackson's Silver and Gold Marks of England, Scotland and Ireland*, rev. edn., Woodbridge, 1989

Voet
Elias Voet, Jr., *Merken van Amsterdamsche Goud- en Zilversmeden*, The Hague, 1912

Voet and van Gelder
Elias Voet and H.E. van Gelder, *Merken van Haagsche goud- en zilversmeden, Haagsche goud- en zilversmeden uit de XVIe en XVIIIe eeuw*, The Hague, 1941

The biographical information on silversmiths is taken from Arthur Grimwade's *London Goldsmiths* unless otherwise credited.

Geometry and the Silversmith

1

Dish

Silver (sterling standard)

London, 1631/32

Maker's mark: RS above a heart and two pellets (Jackson, p. 117, line 18)

Marks: Struck on border with hallmarks (lion passant, leopard's head, date letter) and with maker's mark

Description: Circular with ruled rim, the central well with slightly rising boss in the centre; the border engraved with a lozenge of arms within a wreath; the reverse with scratch weight 61oz-17d

H. 2¼ × Diam. 17¼ in. (5.6 × 44 cm)
Weight: 60 oz. (1862 g)

Heraldry: The arms are those of Twysden impaling those of Finch in a lozenge, as borne by Anne, widow of Sir William Twysden, 1st Bt.

Provenance: Anne, Lady Twysden (d. 1638); the Hon. A.J.F. Mackay of Enterdike, sale, Christie's, London, July 5, 2000, lot 18

Published: Clayton, *Dictionary*, p. 152, plate 231

Before the Restoration in 1660, silver for eating and drinking was divided into two categories: silver for display and drinking, kept on the sideboard or court cupboard, and silver for the table, comprising dishes, plates and salts. Owing to their weight, dishes represented the largest capital expenditure one was likely to make in silver, but only a few sets have survived. The largest group is a service of fifteen dating between 1581 and 1601, found in a Devon potato barn in 1827 and now in the British Museum.[1]

Anne, Lady Twysden became a widow in 1627–28 and died in 1638. She was the daughter of Sir Moyle Finch, 1st Bt. (1550–1614) and had married William Twysden about 1585. Twysden, of Roydon Hall, East Peckham, Kent, had entered Gray's Inn in 1584 and sat as MP for Clitheroe, Helston, Thetford and Winchelsea during a long parliamentary career. He was knighted by James I in 1603 as one of the English gentlemen who had accompanied the king on his progress from Scotland following his accession. In 1611 he was created a baronet. Sir William Twysden was remembered as a great scholar and collector of manuscripts, as was his son, Sir Roger Twysden (d. 1672).

1 See Dora Thornton and Michael Cowell, "The 'Armada Service': A Set of Late Tudor Dining Silver", *The Antiquaries Journal*, vol. 76, 1996, pp. 153–80. A circular deep dish some 14 inches in diameter of 1628/29, mark of Richard Blackwell I, was sold from the Robertson Collection, Christie's, New York, October 27, 1987, lot 449.

2

Tankard

Silver (sterling standard)

London, 1632/33

Maker's mark: BF, three pellets above, trefoil and two pellets below, in shield-shaped punch (Jackson, p. 109, line 9), possibly for Benjamin Francis

Marks: Struck under rim and on top of cover with hallmarks (lion passant, leopard's head, date letter) and with maker's mark

Description: Plain truncated conical with no foot rim, the flat hinged cover with upright scroll thumbpiece formed of rolled sheet, the tubular scroll handle with shield-shaped terminal; the top of the handle pounced NN within a foliate scroll cartouche

H. 6⅞ × W. 5⅞ × D. 4½ in. (17.5 × 15 × 11.5 cm)
Weight: 21 oz. 10 dwt. (669 g)

Provenance: Property of the Rt. Hon. The Earl of Wilton (Sold by Direction of the Court), sale, Christie's, London, July 13, 1921, lot 17; The Choice Collection of Old English and Foreign Silver formed by the late George A. Lockett Esq., sale, Christie's, London, April 22, 1942, lot 81; The Trustees of the Mrs Vera Hue-Williams Property Settlement and the Executors of the estate of Mrs Vera Hue-Williams, sale, Sotheby's, London, March 10, 1994, lot 246

Published: Grimwade, "Tankards", p. 177, fig. 1; Clayton, *History*, p. 61, no. 18

The earliest tankard of this distinct form appears to be one of 1619/20 sold from the Pym Collection, Sotheby's, London, February 6, 1947, lot 166. When sold in 1921, Lord Wilton's collection included this example and a similar one of 1635/36, which also passed into the Lockett Collection. The form is usually thought of as being purely English, but the design was not unknown in France: a gilt example with Paris hallmarks for 1660/61 and the mark of Charles Petit III was presented to the church of Rushbrooke, Suffolk, by the 1st Earl of St Albans.[1]

The body is slightly tapering; the foot has no strengthening ring but is raised from a single piece of silver. The overall design is a form of conceit, for its shape follows the wooden or leather tankards which were probably the commonest form of drinking vessel before cheap salt-glaze stoneware pots from the Rhineland became widespread. A few wooden survivors were excavated from the wreck of the *Mary Rose*, Henry VIII's flagship, which sank off Portsmouth in 1544.[2]

This mark is recorded in the revised edition of Jackson published in 1989 as appearing on small items dating from 1635/36 and 1636/37 and is attributed to Benjamin Francis without a reason being given by the authors. A fluted tazza of 1636/37 with the same maker's mark was sold by Christie's, London, April 12, 1988, lot 287.

The Domcha Collection

Geometry and the Silversmith

When sold in 1994, the Sotheby's catalogue quoted the report on the 1921 sale by the saleroom correspondent of the *Daily Telegraph*: "Silver vessels of the reign of Charles I are scarce, for an obvious reason – most of them had to go into the melting pot for coinage during the Civil War. A few which had escaped appeared at Christie's yesterday, the property of the Earl of Wilton, and probably inherited from the old Egerton family associated with the title. Sold by direction of the court, they were well received … A 1635 Charles I. plain tankard, maker's mark RC with a branch below, realised £343 7s at 420s an oz. (Bateman), the same purchaser giving £364 16s at 340s, for another, 1632, and maker's mark BF with three pellets above and a trefoil and three pellets below." The report refers to the old practice, continued into the 1950s, of conducting the bidding in silver sales at a price per ounce; the purchase price was then computed by multiplying the highest bid by the weight in ounces and pennyweights.

1 Hartop, "Continental", p. 119, fig. 148 and p. 122. I am grateful to Paul Micio for his new identification of the marks on that object.
2 Hartop, "Elizabethan", pp. 306–7.

2

3
Beaker

Silver (sterling standard)

London, 1656/57

Maker's mark: WH, mullet above, pellet in annulet below (Jackson, p. 122, line 3)

Marks: Struck under base with hallmarks (lion passant, leopard's head, date letter) and with maker's mark

Description: Cylindrical with slightly everted rim, on flat base, the side engraved with a coat of arms within ribbon-tied crossed fronds; engraved under the base with the initials *SM*

H. 3¾ in. × Diam. at base: 3 in. (9.5 × 7.6 cm)
Weight: 6 oz. 15 dwt. (208 g)

Heraldry: In heraldic parlance, the arms are "quarterly, 1 and 4, a tree and 2 and 3, a chevron between three martlets". It is not possible to identify them, however, since the tinctures (in other words, colours) are not delineated and without such distinction the coats could belong to a number of families. The systematic representation of tinctures in heraldic engraving, using lines, did not become widespread until the beginning of the eighteenth century.

Provenance: Anonymous sale, Christie's, London, October 27, 1992, lot 401

This maker's mark was attributed by Gerald Taylor to William Harrison I, who was made free in 1646 and admitted to the livery of the Company in 1674. However, another possible candidate is William Hall I of Cheapside, who became a liveryman in 1663 and served twice on the jury of the Trial of the Pyx,[1] in 1664 and in 1679. The mark appears on a significant group of Commonwealth plate, including the twelve-sided porringer and cover of 1655/56 (fig. 6) in the Fogg Art Museum, Harvard University,[2] as well as on more everyday pieces.

A similar beaker of the same date, with the same maker's mark and engraved arms, was formerly in the collection of Charles L. Poor. It has a foot rim, and from its slightly larger proportions it is clear that the two beakers were originally part of a nesting set.[3]

1 The Trial of the Pyx is a ceremony held annually since the Middle Ages at which coins from the Royal Mint are assayed to ensure that they are of the required purity of metal.
2 For a discussion of the possible identity of this maker, see Hartop, *Fogg*, p. 44.
3 Sold Sotheby's, New York, October 26, 2005, lot 119.

4
Goblet

Silver (sterling standard)

London, 1670/71

Maker's mark: PD, three pellets above, cinquefoil below (Jackson, p. 125, line 21)

Marks: Struck on rim with hallmarks (lion passant, leopard's head, date letter) and with maker's mark, under foot with lion passant

Description: On spreading foot rising to a knopped baluster stem and deep bowl; the rim pricked *V* over *NE* over *1671*

H. 5⅝ × Diam. 3⅝ in. (14.2 × 9 cm)
Weight: 7 oz. 10 dwt. (235 g)

Provenance: Sotheby's, London, June 18, 1981, lot 114; Christie's, London, November 23, 1982, lot 108; Christie's, London, May 23, 1990, lot 227

A comparison between this goblet and the two following examples, of 1634/35 and 1654/55, shows the evolution of the shape of the bowl during a forty-year period as it becomes much deeper and almost straight-sided. The capacity also grew over this period.

Commodious goblets of this form were usually referred to as "beer bowls" in contemporary bills and inventories. The 1617 inventory of Abingdon Corporation plate lists "It^m three white beare Bowlls waying Thirtie six ounces and a quarterne".[1] "Beer boules" were among the plate submitted for assay in Dublin in 1638, while the next surviving list of assayed plate at that office, for 1694, records "booze" or "beare cups".[2]

1 Preston, p. 76.
2 Sinsteden, "Assay Records", pp. 144, 148.

4, 5, 6

5
Goblet

Silver (sterling standard)

London, 1654/55

Maker's mark: Cock on reversed C (?) (Jackson, p. 121, line 15)

Marks: Struck on rim with hallmarks (lion passant, leopard's head, date letter) and with maker's mark, under the foot with lion passant

Description: On spreading foot rising to a knopped baluster stem and everted bowl; the side pricked *1663* above *D* over *11*

H. 6⅝ × Diam. 3⅞ in. (17.5 × 10 cm)
Weight: 9 oz. 15 dwt. (303 g)

Provenance: Consul F. C. Reif, Vancouver, Canada, sale, Christie's, London, June 21, 1967, lot 131

A similar goblet of 1650/51 in the Victoria & Albert Museum has what appears to be the same maker's mark struck on it. Philippa Glanville had described that mark as "a bird facing left over a capital D (?) in an oval shield", and the photograph accompanying the catalogue entry does indeed show the mark with what seems to be a D.[1] The impression in Jackson cited above, however, is open on the left side, suggesting a reversed C, and from what can be seen of this mark on the present goblet, it too appears more likely to be a reversed C. Moreover, a goblet of 1655/56 formerly in the Meech Collection was catalogued as having the mark "cock on a reverse C".[2] The mark on the Victoria & Albert Museum cup had been described by Peter Wilding in 1950 as "a weathercock" but any obvious rebuses, or puns, on this symbol are not to be found in recorded silver workers of the time.[3]

1 Glanville, *Tudor and Early Stuart*, p. 413, no. 28.
2 Sotheby's, New York, October 22, 1993, lot 27.
3 Wilding, p. 86.

6
Goblet

Silver (sterling standard)

London, 1634/35

Maker's mark: WC, mullet below, in shaped punch (Jackson, p. 112, line 11)

Marks: Struck on rim with hallmarks (lion passant, leopard's head, date letter) and with maker's mark, under the foot with lion passant

Description: On spreading base rising to a knopped baluster stem and bowl with everted sides

H. 4⅞ × Diam. 3¼ in. (12.5 × 8.3 cm)
Weight: 5 oz. 10 dwt. (171 g)

Provenance: A Connecticut Collector, sale, Sotheby's, New York, April 16, 2005, lot 279

The Domcha Collection

7

7

Six trencher salts

Silver (sterling standard)

London, 1667/68

Maker's mark: TK, fleur-de-lis below, in shield-shaped punch (Jackson, p. 125, line 10)

Marks: Struck in wells with hallmarks (lion passant, leopard's head, date letter) and with maker's mark

Description: Plain circular with spreading sides, central wells; the sides engraved with a crest of a boar, a wreath around its neck, passant

H. 1¼ × Diam. 3¾ in. (3.2 × 9.5 cm)
Weight: 16 oz. 10 dwt. (515 g)

Heraldry: The crest is that of Edgcumbe, probably for Sir Richard Edgcumbe (d. 1688)

Provenance: Probably Sir Richard Edgcumbe (d. 1688), by descent to Kenelm, 6th Earl of Mount Edgcumbe, Mount Edgcumbe sale, Sotheby's, London, May 24, 1956, lot 144; Nathaniel, 3rd Baron Rothschild (1910–1990)

Published: Clayton, *Dictionary*, p. 313, fig. 445

Jackson records this mark on a set of four salts of the same date, and on a sweetmeat dish. It appears on good-quality plate of the 1660s and 70s including an ewer with cut-card work of 1674, formerly in the collection of Lord Bagot.[1]

Pleasantly simple salts of this form are today avidly sought after by collectors, partly for their rarity, although in the seventeenth century they were commonplace. Trencher salts were placed between diners, as opposed to standing salts which were prized for their decorative value and usually positioned in front of the host or principal guest. Edward III had over 500 trencher salts in 1329. Richard Harris gave or bequeathed to Harvard College in the 1640s "One great Salt & one small Trencher Salt" — the trencher salt is gone, but the "great Salt" is what is today known as the Harvard Salt, a larger spool-form version with three vertical scrolls to support a dish.[2] When Samuel Pepys purchased "a dozen of silver salts" on June 19, 1665, paying £6 14s 6d for them, they were obviously trencher salts.

Single examples of trencher salts survive from the beginning of the seventeenth century, and after the Restoration one begins to find pairs or even sets of four, but this one is among the earliest recorded sets of six. A set of six of lobed shape, 1662/63, mark of Christopher Shaw, is in the Untermyer Collection, Metropolitan Museum of Art, New York.[3] They are part of a set of a dozen given to the Company of Painter Stainers by James Heames in 1662.

An identical pair of salts to the Edgcumbe set, of 1665/66, mark *IC above a pellet*, was sold Phillips, New York, March 24, 1983, lot 500, and illustrated in Schroder, *National Trust*, p. 106.

Richard Edgcumbe succeeded his father, a staunch supporter of Charles I, in 1660 and was one of the Knights of the Bath created by Charles II immediately before his coronation in that year. On August 17, 1677 he entertained Charles II to dinner at Mount Edgcumbe, his seat in Cornwall. He died in 1688.

1. Sold Sotheby's, London, May 18, 1967, lot 166, and subsequently Christie's, New York, February 4, 1981, lot 177.
2. For a discussion of the Harvard Salt, and salts in general, see Hartop, *Fogg*, pp. 30–36.
3. Hackenbroch, p. 25, no. 45.

8

Plate

Silver (sterling standard)

London, 1688/89

Maker's mark: IR, crown above quatrefoil below, probably for John Ruslen (Jackson, p. 138, line 15)

Marks: Struck on border with hallmarks (lion passant, leopard's head, date letter) and with maker's mark

Description: Circular with moulded rim, flat border and central well

H. ⅝ × *Diam.* 10¼ in. (1.5 × 28 cm)
Weight: 14 oz. 15 dwt. (462 g)

John Ruslen, trading at the Golden Cup in St Swithin's Lane, was clearly in a large way of business. In addition, he was closely involved with the Goldsmiths' Company, serving as their Prime Warden in 1702 and again in 1707–08. He was patronized by the Jewish community in London, for his mark appears on many of the surviving pieces of Jewish liturgical silver from the period as well as the dishes presented annually to the Lord Mayor by the congregation of Bevis Marks synagogue. He supplied a sanctuary lamp for the synagogue for a total of £37 9s 2d in 1682.[1] Arthur Grimwade remarks of Ruslen that his marks "appear on a number of good quality pieces although there is no suggestion of serious rivalry with the Huguenots".[2]

1 Grimwade, "Anglo-Jewish Silver", p. 114.
2 Grimwade, p. 649.

8

9

Child's "coral" or rattle and teether

Silver (? sterling silver), coral

c. 1690

Maker's mark: WI in script

Marks: Struck on whistle with maker's mark

Description: Octagonal baluster, engraved with stylized leaves, hung with two tiers of bells, the end with whistle, the other end set with a piece of polished coral, the end engraved with the initials *W*B*

H. 1 × W. 5¾ × D. 2 in. (2.5 × 14.6 × 5 cm)
Gross weight: 2 oz. 4 dwt. (69 g)

Coral had long been regarded as having amuletic properties, especially the ability to ward off evil, owing to the fact that it united the three realms of nature: mineral, animal and vegetable. It was only natural that it should be a popular material for a child's teether, although it was not until the second half of the seventeenth century that sufficient quantities were imported into northern Europe to satisfy growing consumer demand.

The word teether is a twentieth-century coinage; it seems that in the seventeenth century they were known simply as "corals". On May 14, 1690 the 1st Earl of Bristol paid Abraham Chambers "for a corail sett in gold £1.10.0."

10

Mug

Silver (sterling standard)

London, 1695/96

Maker's mark: RG, two hexafoils above, one below (Jackson, p. 148, line 9)

Marks: Struck on rim with hallmarks (lion passant, leopard's head, date letter) and with maker's mark

Description: Thistle-shaped on spreading foot, with applied mid-rib and reeded flat scroll handle

H. 3¾ × W. 5 × D. 3⅝ in. (9.5 × 12.6 × 10 cm)
Weight: 7 oz. 15 dwt. (245 g)

Jackson records the same maker's mark on a mug of this date, possibly this one. A similar mug made in London in 1684/85, maker's mark IS, is in the Untermyer Collection, Metropolitan Museum of Art.[1] Thistle-shaped mugs were common in Scotland at this date, but most surviving English mugs have cylindrical bodies.

1 Hackenbroch, p. 37, no. 64.

11

Tumbler cup

Silver (sterling standard)

London, 1692/93

Maker's mark: SD, pellet below (Jackson, p. 142, line 19), possibly for Samuel Dell

Mark: Struck under base with hallmarks (lion passant, leopard's head, date letter) and twice with maker's mark

Description: Plain circular, engraved under the base with the initials *I*N*, the side with late eighteenth-century script initials H over RE

H. 3¼ × *Diam.* 4 in. (8.3 × 10.2 cm)
Weight: 9 oz. 10 dwt. (301 g)

Before 1700, the proportions of tumbler cups tended to be broader than they were to become in the eighteenth century. This example is one of the largest recorded. Tumbler cups and mugs (no. 10) are among the oldest drinking vessels.

9

Geometry and the Silversmith

10, 11

Tumblers are distinguished from beakers (see no. 3) by their ability to right themselves when knocked over. Samuel Pepys records on October 20, 1664: "Thence home, by the way of taking two silver tumblers home, which I have bought …"

12

Twelve dinner plates

Silver (Britannia standard)

London, 1701/02

Maker's mark: Francis Garthorne (Grimwade, no. 736)

Marks: Struck on reverses with hallmarks (Britannia, lion's head, date letter) and with maker's mark

Description: Plain circular, the flat rims moulded on the reverse

H. ½ x *Diam.* 11½ in. (1.4 x 29.2 cm)
Weight: 162 oz. (5044 g)

Provenance: Property of A Collector, sale, Christie's, New York, April 17, 1996, lot 199

The largest capital expenditure on silver one would make during the eighteenth century was for a dinner service. In *service à la française* all the dishes were laid on the table at the start of each of the first two courses.

12

The Domcha Collection

This required a host of serving platters, both elliptical and circular, and at least two dozen dinner plates plus further dishes and plates for the dessert or "banquet" course. Many of the extensive dinner services for which documentation exists had three or four dozen plates to allow for frequent changes by the servants. The weight of silver required was enormous. The Earl of Kildare, whose service survives (see p. 91), paid some £3,669 for a service weighing over 5,000 ounces.

Such sums of money, and the investment required for the raw materials (if the client did not provide all the silver from old plate), posed huge risks for the supplier. Francis Garthorne ran one of the larger workshops producing large-scale plate. He is recorded in St Swithin's Lane between the 1670s and 1726, but he ended his career in old age as "weigher" in the Assay Office, obviously a position given to him out of charity. He died in October 1730.[1] In his heyday, he was one of the Subordinate Goldsmiths to the Jewel Office and produced large-scale works of which these dinner plates are good examples.

1 Grimwade, p. 749.

13

Four trencher salts

Silver (sterling standard)

Dublin, 1707/08

Maker's mark: Thomas Bolton (Bennett, p. 176, no. 477)

Marks: Struck under bases with crowned harp, date letter and maker's mark

Description: Rectangular with canted corners and stepped waisted sides

H. 1 × W. 2⅞ × D. 2¼ in. (2.5 × 7.5 × 5.7 cm)
Weight: 13 oz. 5 dwt. (409 g)

The Dublin date letter upper-case Gothic S is listed as 1706/07 in Jackson, but Ida Delamer and Conor O'Brien, in re-assessing the date letters of the period, have shown that the correct date is 1707/08.[1]

Thomas Bolton was the leading goldsmith and banker in Dublin between the Battle of Boyne and the 1720s. Bolton was elected Lord Mayor of Dublin in 1716.[2] He served as Assay Master from 1693 to 1697, years that saw a tremendous increase in the prosperity of Dublin and the amount of silver assayed there. Bolton's output amounted to approximately a quarter of the total ounces submitted for assay during the 1690s.[3] Dublin assay office records during these years in some cases record the type of objects submitted – in 1694 a total of 219 salts were tested each weighing about 2 ounces. Bolton's work, of which these simple but heavy trencher salts are typical examples, follows the sturdy lines of London-made silver of the day, and it is clear that his workshop often used London-made examples to copy. For example, a Pierre Platel ewer of 1702/03, made for a member of the Gorges family who was Quartermaster General in Cork in that year, was evidently copied by Bolton for an example he supplied as part of a large order of official plate in 1703/04 for the Duke of Ormonde's use as Lord Lieutenant.[4]

1 Delamer and O'Brien, p. 165.
2 Alcorn, *MFA II*, p. 333.
3 Sinsteden, "Assay Records", p. 153.
4 See Sotheby's, London, June 4, 2008, lot 213.

14

Four small candlesticks

Silver (Britannia standard)

London, 1709/10

Maker's mark: John Barnard I (Grimwade, no. 112)

Marks: Struck under bases with hallmarks (Britannia, lion's head, date letter) and with maker's mark, the sockets with lion's head

Description: On square stepped bases with canted corners, rising to knopped stems and cylindrical sockets; the bases engraved in the nineteenth century with a crest

H. 4 × W. 3⅛ × D. 3⅛ in. (10 × 8 × 8 cm)
Weight: 21 oz. 15 dwt. (677 g)

John Barnard was apprenticed to Thomas Dymick in 1677 and was admitted a freeman in 1685. He was one of the signatories to the petition railing against "necessitous strangers" in 1711. The process of sand-casting the components of these candlesticks was laborious but not one that required a great deal of equipment. Innovations which were practised by the immigrant Huguenot workers included lost-wax casting for small delicate components, and it is possible that although Barnard was opposed to foreign competition, he did employ immigrants and that parts of these unusual candlesticks were cast using this process.

Diminutive candlesticks of this type have traditionally been described as "dressing table" candlesticks. This term, however, like so many others used to describe silver today, is probably a twentieth-century invention. The fact that these examples are a set of four suggests that this is an unlikely use for them. Like most objects of the time, these candlesticks were probably intended for use in many contexts.

Geometry and the Silversmith

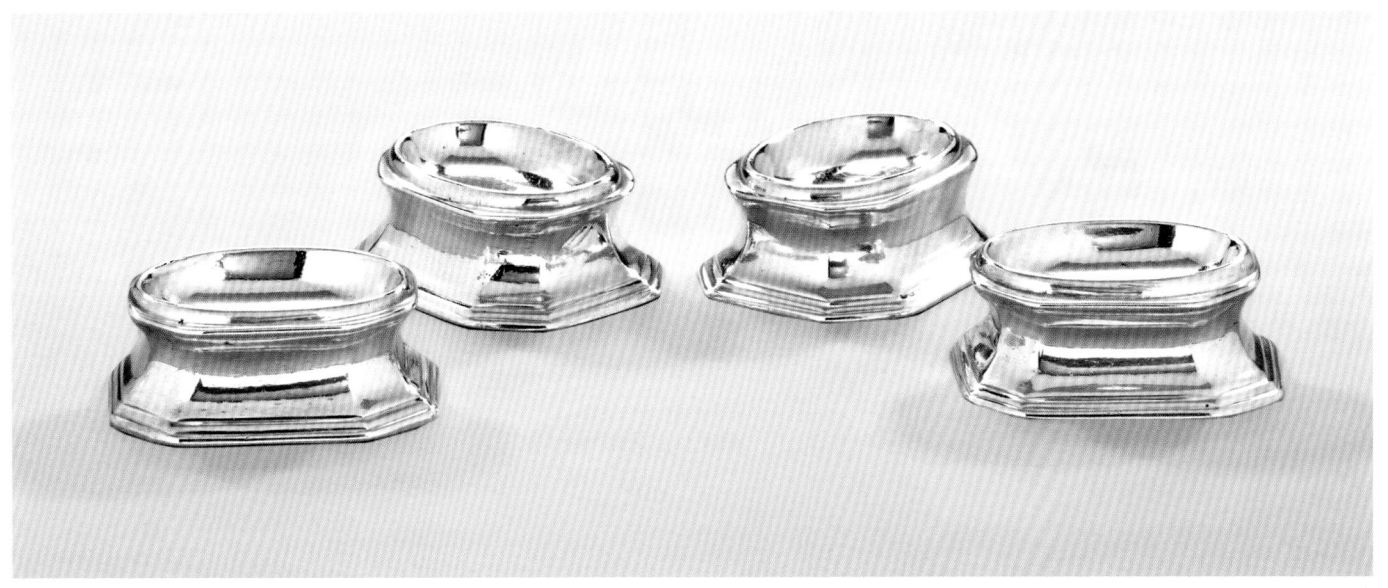

13

14

15, 16

15
Sugar bowl

Silver (Britannia standard)

London, 1709/10

Maker's mark: Seth Lofthouse (Grimwade, no. 1945)

Marks: Struck on side with hallmarks (Britannia, lion's head, date letter) and with maker's mark

Description: Octagonal on spreading octagonal base; the side engraved with a lozenge of arms within a foliate scroll cartouche

H. 2⅜ × *Diam.* 3⅞ in. (6 × 10 cm)
Weight: 5 oz. 15 dwt. (183 g)

Heraldry: The arms appear to be those of Gray impaling those of Chetwynd.

16
Cream jug

Silver (sterling standard)

London, 1720/21

Maker's mark: Edward Vincent (Grimwade, no. 648)

Marks: Struck under foot with hallmarks (lion passant, leopard's head, date letter) and with maker's mark

Description: Octagonal baluster with ruled rim, on spreading octagonal foot, short spout with single drop and flat scroll handle

H. 2⅞ × W. 3 × D. 2 in. (7.3 × 7.6 × 5 cm)
Weight: 3 oz. 10 dwt. (109 g)

This example is among the earliest octagonal cream jugs on a central foot. The type appears to have superseded the octagonal baluster form raised on three scroll feet.

Edward Vincent was in a large way of business with a workshop in the Strand, specializing in tea and coffee wares and large-scale items such as salvers and trays. But his career well shows the perils of the trade at the upper levels, for he appears to have been declared bankrupt twice in his career, the first time in September 1720 on the petition of James Ravener, butcher in Westminster. He re-established his business but found himself insolvent again in 1743.[1]

1 Grimwade, pp. 689–90, 770.

17
Caster or "kitchen pepper"

Silver (sterling standard)

Dublin, 1710/11

Maker's mark: None

Marks: Struck on rim with hallmarks (harp, date letter), interior of cover with harp, traces of maker's mark under base

Description: Cylindrical on reeded foot, with flat scroll handle and slightly domed cover pierced with holes; the front engraved with a crest

H. 2¾ × W. 2⅜ × D. 1⅝ in. (7 × 6 × 4 cm)
Weight: 1 oz. 20 dwt. (61 g)

Heraldry: The crest, that of a wyvern's head, is used by many families.

Geometry and the Silversmith

Provenance: The Collection of Ernest Raphael, sale, Sotheby's, November 8, 1945, lot 18

Published: Sweeney, p. 174, no. 1337

This type of caster is often known as a kitchen pepper or a dredger. It is just as likely that they were used to sprinkle cinnamon as pepper (see notes regarding the larger example, no. 32) and used above as well as below stairs. Two types of pepper were in common use in the eighteenth century, black (*Piper nigrum*) and red (*Capsicum annuum*). White pepper is *Piper nigrum* when ripe, or with the outer skin removed after drying.[1]

1 Bennett, *Trinity*, p. 68.

18

Small saucepan

Silver (sterling standard), fruitwood

London, 1736/37

Maker's mark: George Greenhill Jones (Grimwade, no. 834)

Marks: Struck under base with hallmarks (lion passant, leopard's head, date letter) and with maker's mark

Description: Globular with everted rim and short spout, with straight turned wooden baluster handle; engraved under the base with initials W over GS

H. 3¼ × W. 5 × D. 2¾ in. (8.3 × 12.7 × 7 cm)
Gross weight: 2 oz. 5 dwt. (66 g)

The function of these small pans is unclear. They appear to have acquired the name brandy saucepan in the twentieth century. In the eighteenth century they were sometimes referred to, especially in America, as pipkins or pannekins (a small cooking pot). Surviving examples range in size from two inches in height to massive examples weighing some 60 ounces. Clearly they did not all have the same function. The smaller examples could well have been used for

17

18

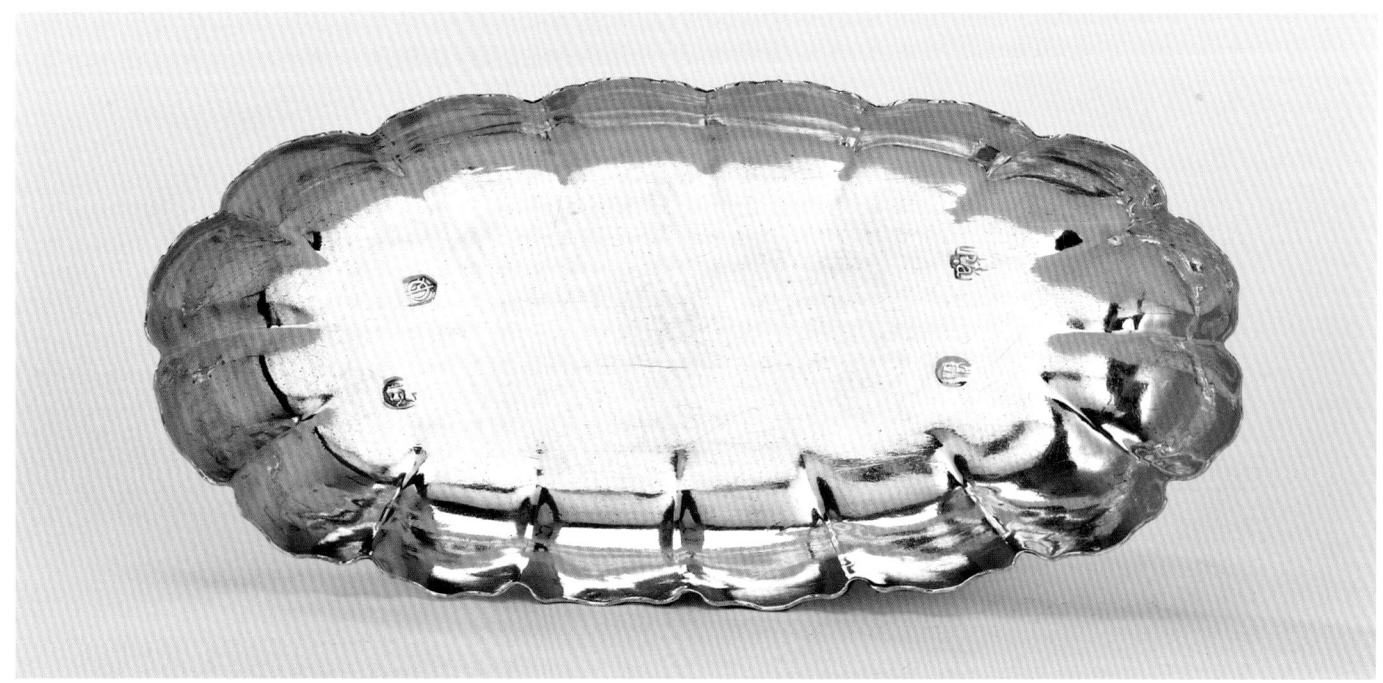

19

warming spirits, but larger examples were most likely used for the preparation of sauces, perhaps in the dining-room itself or even the bedchamber, although the use of silver cooking utensils in the kitchen was not uncommon in aristocratic houses.

19

Spoon tray

Silver (Britannia standard)

London, 1711/12

Maker's mark: Humphrey Payne (Grimwade, no. 2117)

Marks: Struck on reverse with hallmarks (Britannia, lion's head erased, date letter) and with maker's mark

Description: Elliptical with fluted sides and scalloped rim; the reverse engraved TB over P and with scratch weight 3 oz*12 Dwt

H. ¾ x W. 6½ x D. 3⅛ in. (2 x 16.5 x 8 cm)
Weight: 3 oz. 7 dwt. (104 g)

Like so many of his fellow countrymen, Humphrey Payne signed the petitions of 1711 and 1716 against foreign workers. His shop, at the sign of the Hen and Chickens in Cheapside, evidently sold a wide range of plain domestic pieces, usually of the highest quality. The large rectangular tray of 1717/18, no. 22, is among the finest creations of his workshop.

For a discussion of the shape of this dish, see p. 15.

20

20

Hot-milk jug

Silver (Britannia standard), fruitwood

Newcastle, 1717/18

Maker's mark: Francis Batty II (Gill, p. 55, line 7)

Marks: Struck under base with hallmarks (three-tower mark, Britannia, lion's head and date letter) and with maker's mark

Description: Baluster octagonal on spreading octagonal foot, the hinged domed cover with ball finial, the sparrow-beak spout with baluster drop, and ebonized-wood scroll handle at right angles; the front engraved with a crest of a stag's head, under the base with initials *F* over *R A*, and with scratch weight 7:10

H. 5¾ × W. 4 × D. 2¾ in. (14.5 × 10 × 7 cm)
Gross weight: 7 oz. 10 dwt. (234 g)

Heraldry: The crest pertains to a number of families.

The son of Francis Batty I, Francis II was born in 1680–81 and was entered as an apprentice to his father when just two years of age, obviously a formality to enable him to begin working at an early age. He was admitted a freeman of the town in 1701–02 and to the Newcastle Goldsmiths' Company in 1708. Francis I had been elected the first assay master of the company in 1702 and died in 1706, at which point Francis II appears to have taken over his shop called "The Golden Ring".

Goldsmithing was becoming increasingly centralized in London during the early years of the eighteenth century. Many of the provincial assay offices had closed, and shop-keepers had become retailers rather than makers of plate. The trade in Newcastle, however, appears to have thrived for most of the eighteenth century with an assay office serving a wide catchment area. There is no reason to believe that this well-made jug was not made in Batty's workshop, although for many items such as spoons it was cheaper and easier for a provincial maker to buy them ready made from specialist workshops in the capital.

21

Salver

Silver (Britannia standard)

London, 1717/18

Maker's mark: Thomas Mason (Grimwade, no. 1971)

Marks: Struck on field with hallmarks (lion passant, leopard's head and date letter) and with maker's mark, under the base with lion's head

Description: Dodecagonal, with raised border, on circular spool foot with domed base; the centre engraved with a lozenge of arms within foliate scroll and *rocaille*

21

The Domcha Collection

21 coat of arms

H. 3 × W. 10 × D. 10 in. (7.6 × 25.4 × 25.4 cm)
Weight: 25 oz. 15 dwt. (805 g)

Heraldry: The arms are those of Montagu quarterly with those of Monthermer, for a lady of the family of the Dukes of Manchester, or the Earls of Sandwich. The rococo style of the cartouche which surrounds them probably dates from the 1740s.

Polygonal salvers are uncommon. A fifteen-sided example from the workshop of Augustine Courtauld, of 1723/24, formerly in the Clore Collection, was sold from the collection of the Whiteley Trust, Christie's, London, November 22, 2000, lot 183 (fig. 9, p. 16).

22

Tray

Silver (Britannia standard)

London, 1717/18

Maker's mark: Humphrey Payne (Grimwade, no. 2118)

Marks: Struck on field with hallmarks (Britannia, lion's head, date letter) and with maker's mark, each foot with lion's head and maker's mark

Description: Rectangular with rounded corners, raised sides, on four shaped bracket feet; the centre engraved with a baronet's coat of arms within a circular cartouche of scrolling foliage, shells, fish-scale, shells and swags of fruit, the lower part with two architectural plinths supporting recumbent lions, with a lion mask below, and above with two birds, the whole surmounted by a crest and a later baron's coronet

H. 2 × W. 23 × D. 17¼ in. (5 × 58.4 × 43.9 cm)

22

Geometry and the Silversmith

The Domcha Collection

Weight: 157 oz. 10 dwt. (4900 g)

Heraldry: The arms are those of Bridgeman quartering Cradock with Mathews on an escutcheon of pretence, for Sir John Bridgeman, 3rd Bt., born in 1667. He married in 1694 Ursula, daughter and sole heiress of Roger Mathews of Blodwell, Shropshire. He died in 1747.

Provenance: Sir John Bridgeman, 3rd Bt. (1667–1747), by descent to Orlando, 5th Earl of Bradford (1873–1957)

Exhibited: London, 1929, 25 Park Lane, *Loan Exhibition of Old English Plate*, no. 299, lent by the Earl of Bradford (a descendant of Sir John Bridgeman)

Published: Old English Plate, 1929, no. 299

The second decade of the eighteenth century saw the introduction of large salvers, usually oblong, which provided an effective surface on which to engrave elaborate armorials. Unlike large circular chargers, which continued to be made until well into the century, the purpose of these rectangular salvers or trays was not for display, but a practical one of collecting together the newly introduced tea and coffee equipage. This example is among the largest known, and would have fitted neatly onto the top of a rectangular "tea table", a new piece of furniture also recently introduced to the drawing room. Interestingly, there is a geometric foundation to the pleasing proportions of this tray. The depth is exactly 1½ times ½ the width.

The decorative potential of the heraldic engraving continued, however, to be exploited on these "tables". The baroque cartouche enclosing this coat of arms, with its fish-scale, swags and shells supported on an architectural plinth, is similar to the work of Blaise Gentot, a French immigrant engraver who had returned to France by the beginning of the century but who exerted great influence on a generation of heraldic engravers. John Rollos, who was one of a family of goldsmiths and engravers, carried out heraldic engraving for the Jewel Office for a forty-year period until 1744. He specialized in tight circular cartouches formed of scrolling foliage.

For information on Humphrey Payne, see no. 19.

23

Spoon and marrow spoon

Silver (sterling standard)

London, 1717/18

Maker's mark: Nathaniel Roe (Grimwade, no. 2396)

Marks: Struck on back of stem and on marrow scoop with hall-marks (Britannia, lion's head, date letter) and with maker's mark

Description: The tapering cannon handle with removable cap revealing a marrow spoon, the back of the egg-shaped bowl with rat-tail; engraved at the base of the stem with the initials B over EA

H. 1 × W. 16½ × D. 2¾ in. (2.5 × 42 × 7 cm)
Weight: 7 oz. (219 g)

Marrow was standard fare in the eighteenth century, eaten out of the bone with a long scoop, which was often made as the handle of a tablespoon, or, very rarely, as with this example, incorporated into the tubular handle of a spoon.

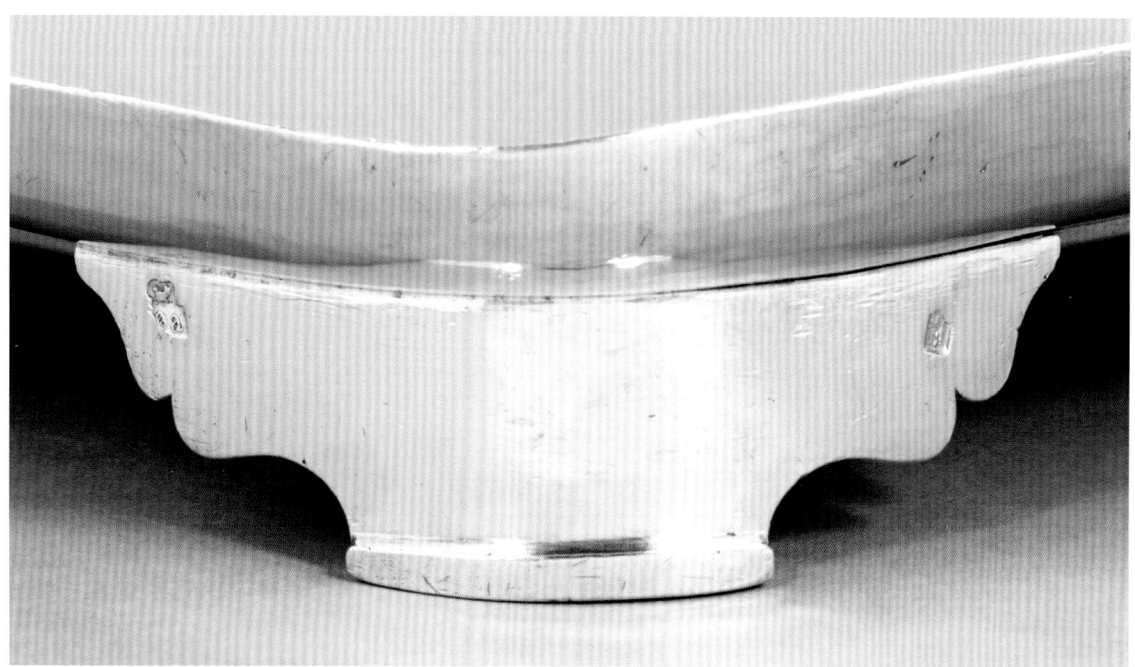

22 foot

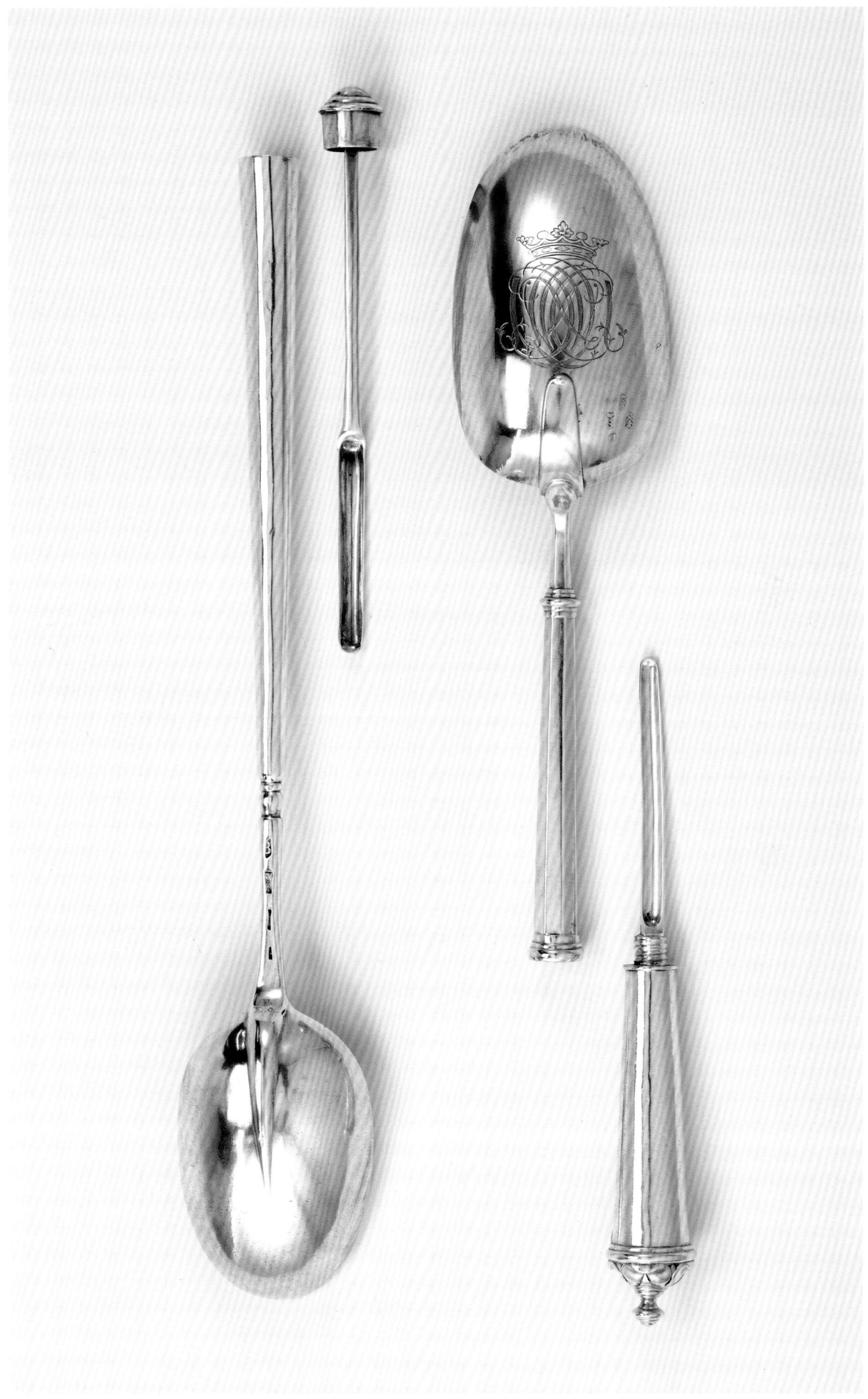

23, 24

For a Dutch example of this type, see no. 24. Marrow spoons appear at the end of the seventeenth century. The most common form after 1700 is double-ended, each end being an elongated scoop of a different size (see no. 66). The term "marrow scoop" is a nineteenth-century one.

Nathaniel Roe was born in Norwich, the son of Matthew Roe, a cutler. His father apprenticed him to the Norfolk-born William Scarlett, a successful spoon maker in Foster Lane, in 1702. Scarlett was a freeman not of the Goldsmiths' Company but the Broderers', and that is probably the reason why Roe became a freeman of that company on completing his apprenticeship in 1710. He entered his first mark, as a largeworker, in that year with an address in Foster Lane.[1] Roe's entry in the Goldsmiths' Company register is annotated "Gon [sic] to live at Norwich", where he was admitted a freeman on November 23, 1717. This spoon may be among the last wares he made in London, or it may have been made in his new shop in Norwich and sent to London for assay, as by then the once-prosperous Norwich assay office had fallen into disuse.

Roe prospered in Norwich and his shop on the Market Place there was probably the largest in the city. In 1724 he was admitted as one of the founder members of Norwich's first Masonic Lodge and in 1727 was appointed a churchwarden of St Peter Mancroft, the city's largest parish church. The civic corporation ordered Roe in 1734 to re-gild the famous Reade Salt and to "melt down the 2 belly potts, 6 salvers, five pottingers and & Salts & 6 spoons", all outmoded pieces of civic plate, and replace them with more modish sauce-boats, salvers, salts and spoons. Some of the items remain in Norwich's civic plate – the sauce-boats bear London hallmarks for 1735/36 and the mark of Joseph Sanders, and the salts the mark of James Smith, so it is clear that by then Roe was primarily a retailing silversmith. Roe married Anna, the daughter of the German immigrant artist John Theodore Heins who worked in Norwich. Roe's will was made in 1757 and proved in 1760.[2]

1 Grimwade, p. 644.
2 Hartop, "Norwich", p. 79.

24

Spoon and marrow spoon

Silver (934/1000 standard)

Amsterdam, 1738/39

Maker's mark: Johannes Koop (Voet, no. 390)

Marks: Struck on the back of the bowl with hallmarks (crowned lion, town mark, date letter) and with maker's mark, the stem with crowned lion and maker's mark

Description: With tapering cannon handle with stylized leaf terminal, unscrewing to reveal a marrow spoon, the lower part octagonal, the back of the egg-shaped bowl with plain tongue; the back of the bowl engraved with a mirrored cipher under a coronet

H. 2 × W. 16¼ × D. 3 in. (5 × 41.2 × 7.6 cm)
Weight: 9 oz. 15 dwt. (304 g)

This Dutch spoon follows the form of English spoons of the period and shows the interchange of design between the two countries during this period. For information on marrow spoons, see no. 23.

25

Spoon

Silver (Britannia standard)

London, 1701/02

Maker's mark: Henry Greene (Grimwade, no. 878)

Marks: Struck on side of bowl with hallmarks (Britannia, lion's head, date letter) and with maker's mark, the back of the stem with lion's head

Description: The tubular cannon handle with baluster terminal, egg-shaped bowl with short rat-tail; the stem engraved with two nineteenth-century crests

H. 1¾ × W. 14¼ × D. 2¾ in. (4.5 × 36.2 × 7 cm)
Weight: 5 oz. (157 g)

Heraldry: The crests pertain to a number of families.

With its elongated bowl and tubular handle, this spoon follows the usual form of the period 1680–1720. Large spoons of this form were made into the 1720s, when they were replaced by wrought spoons that are enlarged versions of tablespoons, of which no. 26 is a typical example. Generally known as "basting spoons", spoons of this size were in reality all-purpose implements for use in the kitchen or on the dining table. Two, probably of the present form, were inventoried in the Royal Collection in 1721 as "large Plain Ladles for Plum Broth",[1] while John Hervey, 1st Earl of Bristol's accounts in 1700 record: "Paid David Willaume the French silversmith for 2 pottage & 4 ragout spoons £15.15.0".[2] Presumably the ragout spoons were the same proportions as this example, necessary for reaching across the table in *service à la française*, while the pottage spoons were probably ladles.

1 Snodin, p. 35.
2 Hayward, p. 83.

26
Spoon

Silver (Britannia standard)

London, 1710/11

Maker's mark: Thomas Sadler (Grimwade, no. 2466)

Marks: Struck on back of stem with hallmarks (Britannia, lion's head, date letter) and with maker's mark

Description: With ribbed upturned stem and egg-shaped bowl with rat-tail; the terminal engraved with a crest, the back of the stem with scratch weight *10"7*

H. 2 × W. 16¼ × D. 3 in. (5 × 41.2 × 7.6 cm)
Weight: 10 oz. 5 dwt. (319 g)

Heraldry: The crest is unidentified.

Provenance: Property of a Gentleman, sale, Christie's, London, November 23, 1999, lot 251

Thomas Sadler entered a mark as a large-worker in 1701 but appears to have been a specialist spoon maker as was his master, Lawrence Coles, to whom he had been apprenticed in 1692.[1]

1 Kent, *Spoonmakers*, p. 34.

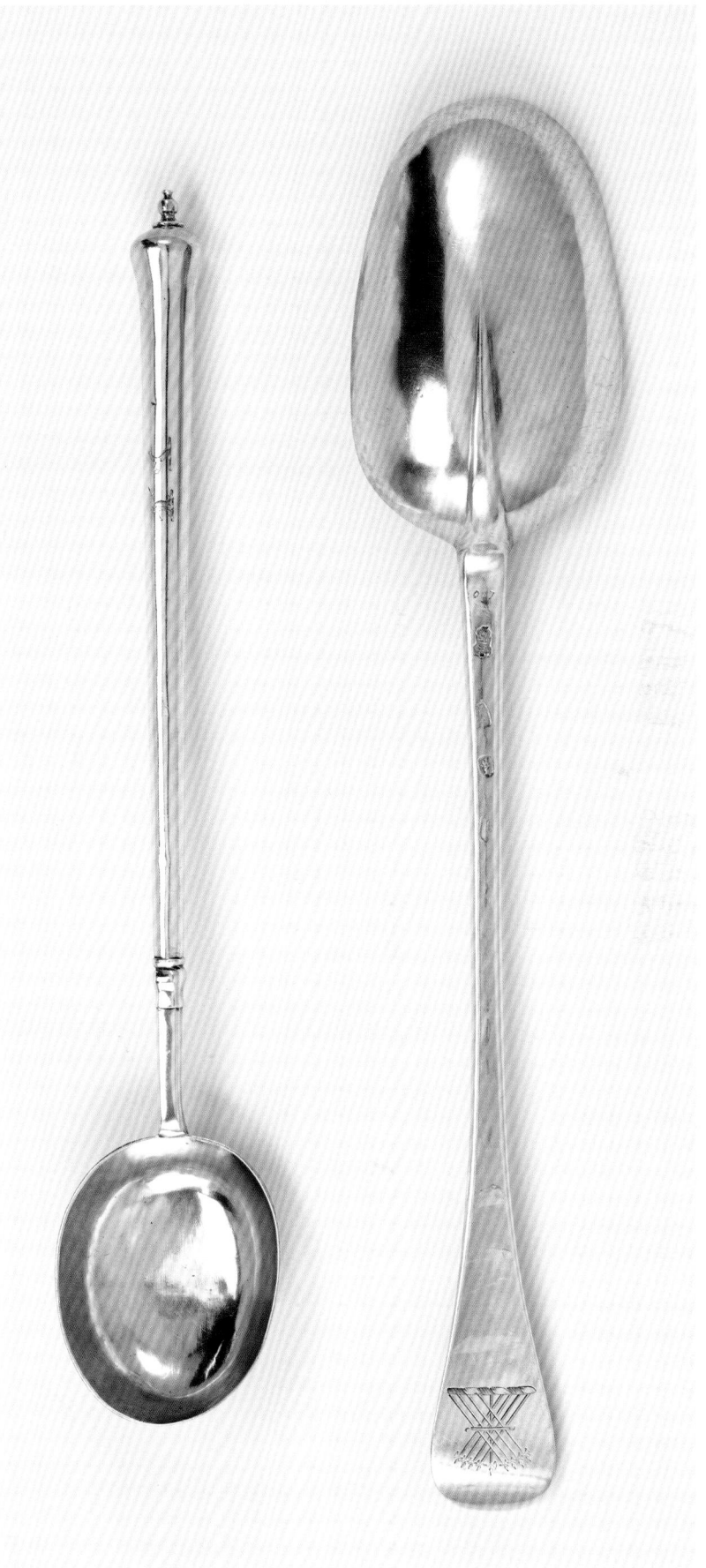

25, 26

27

27

Pair of tapersticks

Silver (Britannia standard)

London, 1718/19

Maker's mark: Joseph Bird (Grimwade, no. 177)

Marks: Struck under bases with hallmarks (Britannia, lion's head, date letter) and with maker's mark

Description: On domed hexagonal bases rising to hexagonal baluster stems and vase-shaped sockets; the bases engraved with a crest

H. 4¾ × W. 3⅜ × D. 3 in. (12.2 × 8.5 × 7.6 cm)
Weight: 9 oz. (280 g)

Heraldry: The crest, that of a martlet flanked by two plumes, is unidentified.

Joseph Bird's mark appears on candlesticks and other lighting equipment, usually of the highest quality. Although he was one of the signatories of the petition railing against immigrant "necessitous strangers" in 1716, he probably employed foreign craftsmen, either as journeymen in his workshop, or as outworkers. In addition to cast baluster candlesticks of this well-known form, he also produced highly unusual examples, such as a pair of square-based candlesticks formed of cast openwork leaves which bear his mark only and are probably the work of a Huguenot immigrant.[1] His mark also appears on a set of triangular-based candlesticks and matching snuffer stand, 1700/01 and 1701/02, elaborately chased with foliage and scrolls, in the Farrer Collection, Ashmolean Museum.[2]

1 With Koopman Rare Art Ltd., London, 2006.
2 Jones, *Farrer*, p. 24.

Geometry and the Silversmith

28

Sugar box

Silver (Britannia standard)

London, 1718/19

Maker's mark: John Chartier (Grimwade, no. 321)

Marks: Struck under base with hallmarks (Britannia, lion's head, date letter) and with maker's mark, the cover flange with lion's head, the interior of the cover with maker's mark

Description: Bowed rectangular with canted corners, on spreading foot, the hinged domed cover with octagonal ball finial; the front engraved with a circular coat of arms within a foliate scroll cartouche flanked by two birds, engraved under the base with scratch weight *15=14=0*

H. 4³⁄₈ × W. 4¹⁄₄ × D. 3¹⁄₂ in. (11.2 × 11 × 9 cm)
Weight: 15 oz. 8 dwt. (479 g)

Heraldry: The arms appear to be those of Aston, baronets (extinct 1815), impaling those of another.

Provenance: Property of a Nobleman, sale, Christie's, London, May 12, 1993, lot 116

The finial on this sugar box is from the same mould as those on the two smaller casters of 1719/20, which also bear Chartier's mark (no. 33). Octagonal sugar boxes enjoyed a brief vogue during the reign of George I. Similar examples to this include one of 1716/17, mark of James Fraillon, in a private collection and one of 1713/14, mark of Pierre Platel, in the Farrer Collection, Ashmolean Museum.[1]

1 See Hartop, *Fogg*, p. 117, nn. 4–5.

29

Saucepan

Silver (sterling standard), fruitwood

London, 1718/19

Maker's mark: Samuel Wastell (Grimwade, no. 2990)

Marks: Struck under base with hallmarks (lion passant, leopard's head, date letter) and with maker's mark

Description: Baluster with moulded rim, spout with drop below and straight turned wooden baluster handle, the socket issuing from a cartouche-shaped panel of cut-card work; engraved under the base with the initials R*M

H. 6 × W. 12½ × D. 7 in. (15.2 × 31.8 × 17.8 cm)
Gross weight: 21 oz. 10 dwt. (666 g)

Provenance: Sotheby's, London, February 27, 1992, lot 369

Samuel Wastell, from King's Lynn in Norfolk, was apprenticed to Benjamin Braford in 1694 and in 1699 was turned over to John Fawdery. Wastell's work, like that of his master Fawdery, is mostly of tea wares of good quality.

30

Caster or "wig duster"

Silver (Britannia standard)

London, 1719/20

Maker's mark: William Bellassye (Grimwade, no. 160)

Marks: Struck under base with hallmarks (Britannia, lion's head, date letter) and with maker's mark, the interior of the cover struck twice with maker's mark

Description: Cylindrical with moulded borders and reeded flat scroll handle, the removable domed cover pierced with holes; the base engraved with scratch weight 5*15

H. 3⅞ × W. 4 × D. 2¾ in. (10 × 10.2 × 7 cm)
Weight: 6 oz. 10 dwt. (201 g)

Utilitarian casters raise questions as to their function. The large size of this example suggests it was used for cinnamon, or flour, or possibly for dusting wigs. Michael Clayton first suggested that such large-size casters might have been intended for use with hair or wig powder and were forerunners of a rare implement of about 1800 which, formed as a tapering cylinder surmounted by a tube, were used to

31, 32

powder wigs.[1] If these casters had a culinary use, they might have been used either above stairs or in the kitchen. The use of silver for kitchen utensils was widespread in the larger households. With gold, silver was thought to be one of the purest materials, although the scientific reasons for its aseptic nature were unknown. In the inventory of Royal Plate undertaken in 1721, an extensive list of silverware under the heading "Kitchen" appears, including a "meat Pott", "8 stew pans & Covers", "cullenders", "kettles" and various spoons and skimmers.[2]

1 Clayton, *Dictionary*, p. 459.
2 NA [PRO]/LC9/66.

31

Caster or "kitchen pepper"

Silver (Britannia standard)

London, 1718/19

Maker's mark: George Greenhill Jones (Grimwade, no. 1563)

Marks: Struck under base with hallmarks (Britannia, lion's head, date letter) and with maker's mark, the exterior of the cover with lion's head and Britannia

Description: Octagonal on stepped base, with applied horizontal rib, reeded flat scroll handle, the removable stepped cover pierced with stylized flowers and with ball finial; the front engraved with a mirrored cipher

H. 3¾ × W. 2⅞ × D. 2⅛ in. (9.5 × 7.3 × 5.5 cm)
Weight: 3 oz. 5 dwt. (98 g)

George Greenhill Jones appears to have specialized in small items such as casters. He was apprenticed to James Goodwin in 1711 and became a freeman of the Goldsmiths' Company on December 3, 1719, entering his first mark, which appears on this caster, on December 5. This object therefore dates from his first five months of business as the date letter changed the following May.

32

Caster or "kitchen pepper"

Silver (Britannia standard)

London, 1716/17

Maker's mark: John Jones I (Grimwade, no. 1564)

Marks: Struck on flange with hallmarks (Britannia, lion's head, date letter) and with maker's mark, under the base and on the exterior of the cover with lion's head and Britannia

Description: Octagonal baluster on stepped base, reeded flat scroll handle, the removable stepped cover pierced with stylized flowers and with octagonal ball finial; engraved under the foot with the initials *IE*

H. 4 × W. 2⅜ × D. 1½ in. (10 × 6 × 3.9 cm)
Weight: 2 oz. 15 dwt. (82 g)

John Jones, the son of Richard Jones, a farrier, was apparently no relation of George Greenhill Jones (see no. 31). His business seems not to have prospered in the same way as his namesake's, and his mark appears infrequently on objects. He was apprenticed to James Seabrook on August 3, 1715 and turned over to Matthew Cooper I to finish his term of apprenticeship on February 1, 1719–20. He was admitted a freeman in 1722 and registered his first mark in 1723. Grimwade records that he was working at an address in Foster Lane in 1719 and surmises "that at or soon after the time he was turned over to Matthew Cooper he was working openly before obtaining his freedom".[1] This is borne out by the presence of his mark on this caster hallmarked for 1716/17.

1 Grimwade, p. 564.

33

Set of three casters

Silver (Britannia standard)

London, 1719/20

Maker's mark: John Chartier (Grimwade, no. 321)

Marks: Struck under bases with hallmarks (Britannia, lion's head, date letter) and with maker's mark, the exterior of the covers with lion's head, two also with maker's mark

Description: Comprising a large and a pair of smaller examples, each baluster octagonal on spreading foot, the bayonet-fitting fluted high-domed covers pierced with panels of stylized scrolls, vases and flowers, with octagonal ball finial; the interiors of the two smaller covers with later fitted sleeves, the larger engraved under the base with scratch weight *26=8*

The larger example:
H. 7⅞ × Diam. 3⅛ in. (20 × 8 cm)

The smaller examples:
H. 5⅞ × Diam. 2¼ in. (15 × 5.6 cm)

Weight: 27 oz. (845 g)

Provenance: Sotheby's, New York, April 7, 1987, lot 175

Sets of casters, comprising a pair of small and a larger single example, became widespread from the 1680s onwards. The first examples were cylindrical with high-domed covers but by the first decade of the eighteenth century the baluster form, which would be used for cream jugs and coffee pots as well, became the preferred form. The curving interior of the body allowed for easy cleaning. Piercing on the high-domed covers of these casters was often imaginative, as on these examples, incorporating stylized vases formed of foliate scrolls, laboriously cut out with fine-toothed fret saws.[1] Patterns of this sort of ornament were readily available in French or even English pattern books such as Simon Gribelin's *A New Book of Ornaments*, published in London in 1704.

It is evident that these sets of casters were used for sprinkling ground substances on food, but what these were is still the cause of some debate among silver scholars and food historians. The price of sugar continued to fall following the development of sugar plantations in the New World during the second half of the seventeenth century, and it seems most likely that the larger caster was for sugar chipped off a cone and ground. In the early eighteenth century, dinner services were divided between components in white silver, used for the first two courses, and a silver-gilt portion used for the dessert or "banquet" course. The service issued to the Earl of Chesterfield by the Jewel Office in 1727 included, in the dessert portion, a pair of large octagonal gilt casters which were no doubt for sugar. But sugar was also sprinkled onto savoury foods, and triads of casters were often fitted to the novel *surtouts de table* that appeared on fashionable London tables from the 1720s onwards.[2] Further down the social scale, the all-purpose "cruet stand" made in large quantities from the 1730s onwards usually included a triad of casters as well as bottles for oil and vinegar.[3]

Among the possible contents of the two smaller casters are mustard and ground pepper, the latter usually found during this period in two varieties, black and cayenne (both of which also fell dramatically in price during the period). A notice of stolen goods in the *London Gazette* in 1687 lists "A Sugar-Box, a Pepper-Box, and a Mustard-Box, without mark", suggesting a triad of casters. In 1689 William Fitzhugh of Virginia ordered through his agent in London "a Sett of Castors that is to say for Mustard, Pepper & Sugar about 24 or 26 ounces".[4] However, the idea prevalent among silver writers that mustard was sprinkled as a powder on to meats is not documented. In the Middle Ages, sugared mustard was a popular sauce for partridge, pheasant and rabbit, and as early as 1609 Sir Hugh Plat in his *Delights for Ladies* speaks of "our mustard which we buy from the chandlers at this day is many times made up with vile and filthy vinegar, such as our stomack would abhore if we should see it before the mixing thereof with the seeds".[5] In a description of a London cook-shop, the forerunner of a restaurant, written by a French visitor in 1719, mustard is mentioned, made up in what appears to be the modern paste version: "… with this, a little Salt and Mustard upon the Side of a Plate, a Bottle of Beer and a Roll; and there is your whole Feast".[6] An advertisement in the *London Journal* for August 31, 1723, declares: "The Royal Flower of Mustard Seed is now used and esteemed by most of the Quality and Gentry … and one spoonful of the Mustard made of it will go as far as three of that sold at chandlers' shops, and is much wholesomer".[7]

Some silver casters have covers that are in fact "blind" with engraved decoration to match the piercing on the other

33

covers in the set, suggesting that mustard was served as the paste we know today. Many of these "blind" covers were pierced in the early twentieth century when the antique-silver trade responded to the demand for pepper "shakers" on the table. In 1724 Horatio Walpole was issued a dinner service by the Jewel Office which included:

	oz.	dwt.	gr.
Two casters	52	3	0
Four cruett tops, 4 cruett glasses, & 2 mustard glasses	14	16	0
Two cruet frames, 2 Mustard Barrels, & 2 spoons	109	10	0[8]

Walpole's "mustard barrels", which have survived and bear the mark of Jacob Margas and London hallmarks for 1724/25, are early versions of the late Georgian mustard pot intended for serving mustard paste.[9] In a 1751 list of plate sent to the Earl of Orford are "sugar pepper and mustard casters",[10] but by the third quarter of the century the vase for mustard paste was rapidly being replaced by the mustard pot (see no. 84) and triads of casters were no longer made.

1. For a description of the process, based on the observations of Ubaldo Vitali, see Micio, p. 30, n. 4.

2. The term "triad" was used by Peter Thornton to describe seventeenth-century sets comprising a looking-glass, table and *guéridons* and it seems appropriate to use it for these sets of casters (Thornton, p. 94).

3. Among the earliest of the "Warwick" form is one of 1735/36 with the mark of Chartier, sold Sotheby's, New York, June 4, 1974, lot 64.

4. Davis, p. 148.

5. Brett, *Dinner*, p. 48.

6. *M. Misson's Memoirs and Observations in His Travels over England*, translated from the French by Mr Ozell, 1719, quoted in Drummond, *Food*, p. 105.

7. Godfrey, p. 12.

8. NA [PRO]/LC/44/f. 169.

9. Sold by a descendant of Horatio Walpole, Sotheby's, London, June 1, 2000, lot 186.

10. Cambridge University Library/Cholmondeley MSS/Ch(H)A/C/39/2.

34

Strainer

Silver (Britannia standard)

London, 1719/20

Maker's mark: George Gillingham (Grimwade, no. 832)

Marks: Struck in the centre with hallmarks (Britannia, lion's head, date letter) and maker's mark, the reverse of each handle with lion's head

Description: Octagonal with stepped sides, pierced with panels of stylized flowers; the two flat shaped handles pierced and engraved with scrolls

H. 1 × W. 7 × D. 3 in. (2.5 × 17.8 × 7.6 cm)
Weight: 2 oz. 2 dwt. (68 g)

Provenance: H. A. Cooper, 1967

Published: Delieb, p. 54

Two-handled strainers of this type were popular during the first quarter of the eighteenth century and were most likely used with small punch-bowls of silver or ceramic. The same handle design appears on strainers with the mark of John Albright, such as the example of 1719/20 sold Sotheby's, New York, October 22, 2002, lot 622, and two of 1718/19, both mark of John Albright and William Looker, illustrated in Bernard Crewdson, "Silver Strainers, a Little-known Field for a Collector" in *Connoisseur*, May, 1950, p. 108, fig. X. The author of this article surmises, probably correctly, that the piercing of this type of strainer was probably done by one specialist workshop. Their function was probably to strain lemon and orange juice into punch; an inventory of plate at Knole in Kent made in 1665/66 lists "A little Cullender for oranges".[1]

1 West Kent Record Office/Sackville Papers/U269/E79.

35

Four candlesticks

Silver (Britannia standard)

London, 1719/20

Maker's mark: Thomas Parr I (Grimwade, no. 2120)

Marks: Struck under bases with hallmarks (Britannia, lion's head, date letter) and with maker's mark, the socket with lion's head

Description: On domed octagonal bases rising to knopped baluster octagonal stems and vase-shaped sockets; the bases engraved with a lozenge of arms within a foliate scroll cartouche

H. 5½ × W. 3⅞ × D. 3⅞ in. (14 × 9.8 × 9.8 cm)
Weight: 49 oz. 12 dwt. (1543 g)

Heraldry: The arms are those of a lady of the Armine family, Osgodby, Lincolnshire.

Thomas Parr, the son of a Cork clergyman, was apprenticed to Simon Noy in 1687 and admitted a freeman in 1694. He registered a mark as a largeworker, giving an address in Wood Street, and later moved to Cheapside. He signed both the petition in 1711 complaining about the competition

34

35

of the "necessitous strangers" and the one in 1716 against assaying the work of foreigners who had not served a seven-year apprenticeship. His work, mostly candlesticks and well-made tea wares, shows the use of skilled sand- and lost-wax casting, and it is evident that he was among the high-level English manufacturers of his time.

36
Salver

Silver (Britannia standard)

London, 1719/20

Maker's mark: John Pero (Grimwade, no. 2171)

Marks: Struck on reverse with hallmarks (Britannia, lion's head, date letter) and with maker's mark

Description: Octofoil formed of elliptical arcs and with raised rim, on four bracket feet; the centre engraved with a coat of arms, motto and earl's coronet within a foliate scroll and architectural cartouche, the rusticated plinth with two wild-man supporters; engraved on the reverse with scratch weight *49=15*

H. 1¾ x W. 14 x D. 14 in. (4.5 x 35.5 x 35.5 cm)
Weight: 48 oz. (1492 g)

Heraldry: The arms are "quarterly, 1 and 4, a lion rampant gules, armed and langued azure" for Viscount Macduff and Earl Fife and, "2 and 3, vert a fess dancetty between a hart's head cabossed in chief and two escallops in base or" for Duff of Braco, impaling those of Grant, as borne by William Duff, created Earl Fife in 1759.

Provenance: William Duff, 1st Earl Fife (c. 1696–1763), then by descent to his youngest son Arthur Duff, who at his death in 1805 left his estate to his nephew, Richard Wharton (subsequently Duff), son of Lady Sophia, fifth daughter of the 1st Earl Fife and Thomas Wharton, then by descent to their youngest child Jemima (b. 1815), who married John Robert Tod, then by descent to their only daughter Anne Helen (b. 1843), who married Edward Chancellor, then by descent to Sir Christopher Chancellor CMG, sale, Christie's, London, December 10, 1958, lot 76; Mrs Fay Plohn, New York, sale, Sotheby's, London, July 16, 1970, lot 59, M.P. Levene Ltd., Hilmar Reksten, sale, Christie's, London, May 22, 1991, lot 112

Published: Dixon, p. 20

William Duff succeeded to the Perthshire estate of Braco on the death of a cousin in 1719 and this salver no doubt formed part of the plate ordered at this time. Three years later he inherited his father's Banffshire estates worth some £6,500 a year. He was a loyal servant of the Hanoverians although he was one of the small group of anti-Walpole Whigs which

The Domcha Collection

36

included Lord Hardwicke, the Duke of Bedford and Earl Fitzwalter (see no. 73). He sat as MP for Banffshire between 1727 and 1735 in which year he was created Baron Braco of Kilbryde. Ten years later he refused to support the Jacobite uprising. In 1759 he was created Earl Fife in the peerage of Ireland.

Duff married Janet, the widow of Hugh Forbes and daughter of the Earl of Findlater. After her death in 1720 he took as his second wife Jean, second daughter of Sir James Grant of Colquhoun.

During his lifetime Duff purchased considerable estates in the shires of Aberdeen, Banff and Moray, and in about 1724 he started work building a new castle at Balvenie. Then in 1730 he commissioned William Adam to design an imposing mansion in the Palladian style to be known as Duff House. It is, according to John Dunbar, "the most arresting of all Adam's surviving major works; a medieval castle in Baroque dress, its rich texture and towering bulk convey a memorable impression of seignorial pomp".[2] The dramatic verticality of the central block of Duff House owes much of its impact to the use of hewn freestone. But the stone was also to be the cause of dramatic cost overruns, largely because much of it was shipped ready worked, at great expense, from Adam's quarries on the Firth of Forth. There ensued an acrimonious lawsuit between Duff and Adam. The main block, begun in 1735, was finally roofed in 1739 but the wings were still uncompleted at the time of Duff's death and it is said that the laird harboured such bad feeling for the house that he never set foot in it, and ordered his carriage blinds to be drawn as he passed it.[3]

The arms on the shield in the achievement on this salver show signs of having been re-engraved. This is explained by

William Duff, Lord Braco, later Earl Fife (c.1696–1763) by William Smith, oil on canvas, reproduced in Tayler, facing p. 114. *Syndics of Cambridge University Library*

the fact that William Duff's first wife died in 1720 and her arms on the right hand of the shield were re-engraved with his new wife's arms when he married her in 1723.[4] In that year, on July 19, he registered his arms and had a further grant from the Lyon Office of two wild men as supporters of the shield, and the motto *Virtute et Opera*. Moreover, Duff's arms on the left hand are those he registered on January 22, 1760 shortly after his ennoblement as Earl Fife, which include an additional coat of a lion rampant in the first and last quarter of the shield.[5] The earl's coronet was also added at this time and is replacing the Duff crest, although the torse, or base, of it can be seen under the coronet.

1 The *Dictionary of National Biography* and auction catalogues have erroneously described him as Earl *of* Fife. It was not until 1885 that his descendant was created Earl *of* Fife in the peerage of the United Kingdom.
2 Dunbar, p. 110.
3 Gifford, p. 155.
4 This salver is one of a pair; the other is in a private American collection. The same armorials appear on a two-handled cup and cover of 1723/24, mark of James Fraillon, sold as The Property of a Gentleman, Christie's, London, November 28, 1979, lot 102, Sotheby's, New York, December 15, 1983, lot 196, and again Sotheby's, New York, October 19, 1995, lot 458.
5 Tayler, p. 567.

36 achievement

The Domcha Collection

37

38

37

Sugar bowl and cover

Silver (Britannia standard)

London, 1719/20

Maker's mark: John Sanders I

Marks: Struck on side with hallmarks (Britannia, lion's head, date letter) and with maker's mark, the cover flange with lion's head and maker's mark

Description: Octagonal on spreading octagonal base, the high-domed octagonal cover with octagonal baluster finial; the side engraved with a circular coat of arms within foliate scroll mantling and surmounted by a crest; the cover with the same crest

H. 5¾ × W. 5⅛ × D. 5⅛ in. (14.6 × 13 × 13 cm)
Weight: 18 oz. 5 dwt. (570 g)

Heraldry: The arms are those of Bagot.

John Sanders was admitted a freeman in 1715 and entered his first mark as a largeworker in 1717. He is recorded working as late as 1748. He does not appear to have had retail premises but supplied others with wares. He was one of the signatories of the petition in 1716 complaining about foreigners not having served seven years' apprenticeship.

38

Pair of fluted dishes

Silver (Britannia standard)

London, 1719/20

Maker's mark: David Willaume I (Grimwade, no. 3194)

Description: Circular on rim feet, chased with twenty radiating flutes under a scalloped rim; the rim engraved with a heraldic badge enclosed by the Order of the Garter surmounted by a duke's coronet

H. ⅞ × Diam. 5¾ in. (2.3 × 14.6 cm)
Weight: 15 oz. 15 dwt. (490 g)

Heraldry: The badge is that used by the Pelham family, borne in this context by Thomas Pelham, later Pelham-Holles, 1st Duke of Newcastle-upon-Tyne (1693–1768).

Provenance: Thomas Pelham, later Pelham-Holles, 1st Duke of Newcastle-upon-Tyne (1693–1768)

Fluted circular dishes of this small size were usually referred to as "saucers" in the eighteenth century and it is most likely they were set on the dining table between the larger dishes and platters and used for serving sauces or sweetmeats. With the advent of the epergne in the next decade, similar dishes were often fitted to satellite branches to raise them up off the tabletop. Small circular dishes are also found in documents referred to as counter trays, no doubt used for gaming counters. A slightly larger pair of similar dishes from Willaume's workshop, of the same date, was sold Bonhams, London, July 4, 2007, lot 205.

For information about the 1st Duke of Newcastle, and about the use of larger fluted dishes, see no. 60. The use here of the Pelhams' heraldic badge rather than their crest is interesting. Badges were devices borne by heads of great families and have existed since the Middle Ages alongside coats of arms and crests with which they are often confused. Badges are not governed by the laws of heraldry. The Pelham badge of a buckle (from a sword belt) is said to have been granted to a Pelham for bravery at the Battle of Poitiers in 1356, but this is probably a seventeenth-century romantic fabrication. It was, however, used by the family from the fifteenth century onwards, often as a livery, or servant's, badge.[1]

1 A silver-gilt two-handled covered cup of 1707/08, with the mark of David Willaume I, was sold from the collection of Mrs J. H. Dent-Brocklehurst, Sotheby's, London, May 2, 1963, lot 58.

39

Flask

Silver (? sterling standard), glass

c. 1720

Maker's mark: George Meale of London (Grimwade, no. 848)

Marks: Struck under base of cup with maker's mark

Description: Curved oblong with faceted cut-glass body, hinged domed cap engraved with stylized leaves, the lower part with removable elliptical cup with reeded rim, on reeded foot; the cup engraved with a coat of arms within a foliate scroll and rusticated cartouche headed by a shell and, on the other side, with a crest

H. 7 × W. 2⅝ × D. 1⅝ in. (17.8 × 6.5 × 4 cm)
Weight of cup: 1 oz. (31 g)

39 coat of arms

The Domcha Collection

39, 40

Heraldry: The arms are those of Edgar quartering those of Sparrow, for a descendant of Devereux Edgar (1651–1744).

Provenance: Property of a Gentleman, sale, Christie's, London, November 19, 2002, lot 135

Devereux Edgar was the third son of Thomas Edgar, a Recorder of Ipswich, who married Temperance, daughter of Robert Sparrow of Wickhambrook, Suffolk, in September 1681. Edgar was a commissioner for the Justice of the Peace in 1700 but lost his post following a row with the local bailiff whom he called "a lyer, blockhead and a jackanape". Friends of his petitioned the queen on his behalf, alleging that the bailiff had been granting "Freemen" for £6 a time to allow men to avoid being drafted. He was restored as commissioner in 1710.

40
Flask

Silver (? sterling standard), interior gilt

c. 1745

Maker's mark: IW in script, probably for James Wilks of London (cf. Grimwade, no. 1753)

Marks: Struck twice on base and base of cup with maker's mark

Description: Curved oblong, the lower part with removable cup, engraved with a band of pales, with screw-on cover and internal plug; the side engraved with a crest

H. 7¼ × W. 3½ × D. 1½ in. (18.5 × 9 × 3.9 cm)
Weight: 11 oz. 15 dwt. (368 g)
Heraldry: The crest is that of Crome.

This maker's mark is very similar to that registered by James Wilks at Goldsmiths' Hall in 1742 but an exact identification is not possible. Stylistically, the flask dates from the first half of the eighteenth century but there were no workers who registered an *IW in script* mark before John White entered his version, with a star above, in 1739. Another possibility is that it is a mark, hitherto unrecorded, used by a provincial goldsmith.

41
Strainer spoon

Silver (sterling standard), fruitwood

London, 1721/22

Maker's mark: Andrew Archer (Grimwade, no. 1)

Marks: Struck on back of stem with hallmarks (lion passant, leopard's head, date letter) and with maker's mark

Description: With tapering wooden handle with ball terminal, egg-shaped bowl half pierced with holes; the back of the bowl with scratch weight 3=11=0

H. 1½ × W. 17 × D. 2⅜ in. (3.8 × 43.2 × 6 cm)
Gross weight: 4 oz. 10 dwt. (143 g)

42
Ladle

Silver (sterling standard)

London, 1691/92

Maker's mark: William Mathew (Jackson, p. 141, line 4)

Marks: Struck inside bowl with hallmarks (lion passant, leopard's head, date letter) and with maker's mark

Description: The curved tapering cannon handle with baluster finial, the elliptical bowl with short rat-tail; the end of the stem engraved in the nineteenth century with a coat of arms within foliate scroll mantling

H. 2½ × W. 16 × D. 4⅛ in. (6.4 × 40.7 × 10.5 cm)
Weight: 8 oz. 10 dwt. (264 g)
Provenance: The Hahn Family Collection of English Silver, sale, Christie's, New York, October 23, 2000, lot 303

The attribution of this mark to William Mathew has been made by Timothy Kent.[1] Mathew was apprenticed to John Smith in 1675 and admitted a freeman in 1683. He worked in Foster Lane, later moving to George Alley, Lombard Street. With the introduction of the Britannia standard in 1697 he entered a new mark at Goldsmiths' Hall. He was dead by 1707.

1 Kent, *Spoonmakers*, p. 51.

43
Strainer spoon

Silver (sterling standard), fruitwood

London, c. 1720

Maker's mark: William Looker (Grimwade, no. 3219)

Marks: Struck on the side of the bowl with hallmarks (lion passant, leopard's head) and with maker's mark

Description: With turned wooden baluster handle, the egg-shaped bowl half pierced with holes, with short rat-tail

H. 2¼ × W. 17¼ × D. 3 in. (5.7 × 43.8 × 7.6 cm)
Gross weight: 5 oz. 10 dwt. (176 g)
Provenance: The late Lord Bauer, sale, Clarke Gammon Wellers, Guildford, December 10, 2002, lot 584

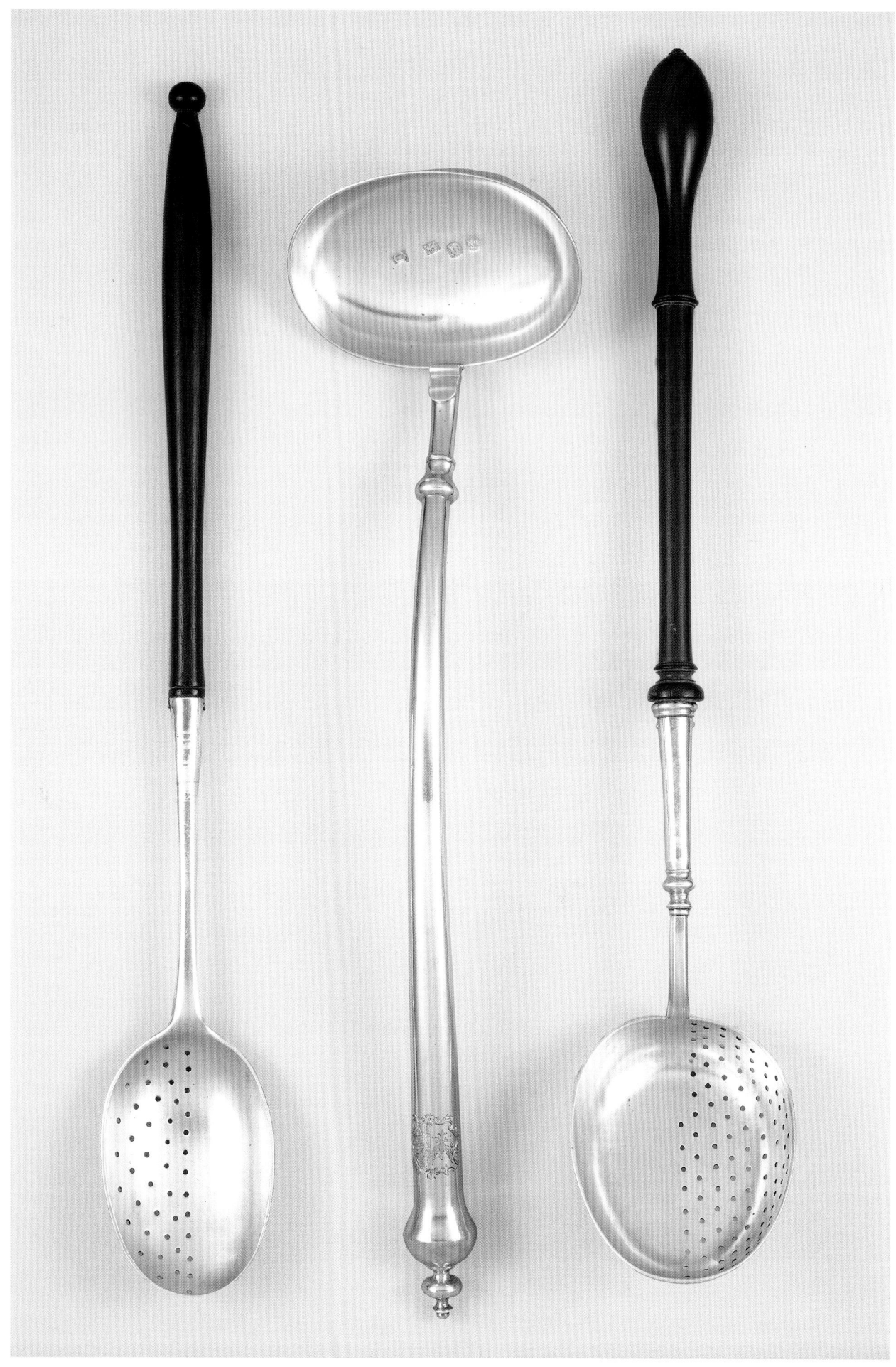

41, 42, 43

44

Teapot

Silver (Britannia standard), fruitwood

London, 1721/22

Maker's mark: Arthur Dicken (Grimwade, no. 474)

Marks: Struck under base with hallmarks (Britannia, lion's head erased, date letter) and with maker's mark, the inside of the cover with lion's head erased

Description: Globular octagonal on octagonal rim foot, the hinged cover with wooden bud finial, tapering octagonal spout and wooden loop handle; one side engraved with a circular coat of arms within foliate scroll mantling and surmounted by a crest

H. 5 × W. 9 × D. 4½ in. (12.7 × 22.8 × 11.4 cm)
Gross weight: 20 oz. (623 g)

Heraldry: The arms are those of Watson, of Fulmer, Buckinghamshire, baronets.

Provenance: The Palladio Stiftung, Liechtenstein, sale, Christie's, London, June 26, 1974, lot 115

Exhibited: Cambridge, Fitzwilliam Museum, March 15, 1969–March 15, 1970

45

Beer jug

Silver (Britannia standard)

London, 1721/22

Maker's mark: Thomas Farren (Grimwade, no. 666)

Marks: Struck under base with hallmarks (Britannia, lion's head, date letter) and with maker's mark

Description: Baluster on spreading foot, moulded rim and scroll handle, the front engraved with a mirrored cipher within a foliate scroll circular cartouche, engraved under the base with scratch weight 27=7

H. 7⅛ × W. 6¾ × D. 4⅞ in. (18.1 × 17.2 × 12.4 cm)
Weight: 27 oz. (843 g)

Provenance: Walter H. Willson, 1932; How of Edinburgh Ltd.; A Lady, sale, Christie's, London, November 29, 1972, lot 109, Ricardo Espirito Santo Silva, sale, Christie's, London, July 5, 2005, lot 39

Exhibited: London, 1932, *Art Treasures Exhibition*, no. 508

Published: How, *Notes 1946–47*, p. 21, plate 15

45

Thomas Farren, who served as Subordinate Goldsmith to the King between 1723 and 1742, operated one of the most prolific workshops in London during the 1720s and 30s.

The superb quality of this beer jug was appreciated by the dealer and scholar Commander How when he owned it in the 1940s: "I was at home, working on our book, and my wife insisted on my coming to London to see a jug she thought was the best she had ever seen. I went to see it and she awaited my verdict with some anxiety as she was very much excited about the thing but did not want to pay a fantastic price without a corroboratory opinion from me. My only remark when I had seen the piece was that she had grossly underestimated in her description. It was also the finest jug I had ever seen, and I very much doubted if there was a finer or more beautiful George I example still extant. I have to give my wife best here, this jug could not possibly be improved by being octagonal … Heavy as lead, with a perfect surface, in mint condition with mint marks, the lip part and parcel of the rim as opposed to an added spout, I consider it a most remarkable and highly desirable example of George I silver. It has everything that the finest plain silver should have, including a good contemporary cipher within contemporary mantling. I shall be very sorry when it is sold as I greatly enjoy using it myself nearly every day. When plain silver is as fine as this it is indeed difficult to uphold one's defence of the decorated, but this is one of many exceptions which prove the rule, and the absolute tops in this plain silver of the Queen Anne–George I period does indeed take a very great deal of beating – *but it must be the tops*."[1]

1 How, *Notes*, 1946–47, p. 21.

46

Salver

Silver (Britannia standard)

London, 1721/22

Maker's mark: Anthony Nelme (Grimwade, no. 68)

Marks: The field struck in each corner with a hallmark (lion passant, leopard's head, date letter) and maker's mark

Description: Oblong, but with subtle curvature suggestive of a superellipse and with raised sides, on four curved bracket feet; the centre engraved with a lozenge of arms within a foliate scroll and fish-scale cartouche

H. 1½ × W. 11¼ × D. 8⅛ in. (4 × 28.6 × 20.6 cm)
Weight: 31 oz. (723 g)

Heraldry: The arms, which are borne by a lady, appear to be those of Carr or Whiteman impaling those of Darcy or Sepham.

Provenance: Anonymous sale, Christie's, New York, October 18, 1989, lot 130

Plain square or oblong trays such as this example are based on imported Japanese lacquer trays which were often made in graduated sets fitting into each other. A set of six square silver examples of 1719/20, mark of Thomas Folkingham, is in the Untermyer Collection in the Metropolitan Museum of Art, New York.[1] These are graduated into three sizes, making two sets of three which fit into each other.

Anthony Nelme had established one of the biggest workshops in London by the end of the seventeenth century. He was one of the petitioners against the work of "aliens and foreigners" in 1697, although, as Arthur Grimwade has observed, "His work shows some effect of the Huguenot influence and it would seem probable that he had immigrant journeymen working for him, or purchased and overstruck their productions."[2] This is borne out by the fact that in the Court of Aldermen Papers for September 1706 Nelme "lately in extraordinary hast to work up divers parcells of Silver Plate and being at a Loss for a Journeyman in one particular part of Yo^r Peticoners said Trade Did for that purpose entertaine one John Christian Volage a Germane."[3] Nelme died in 1723.

1 Hackenbroch, p. 66, no. 127.
2 Grimwade, p. 606.
3 Reference by Robert Barker, Grimwade, p. 760.

45 cipher

47

Salver

Silver (934/1000 standard)

The Hague, 1722/23

Maker's mark: Adrian Havelaar (Voet and van Gelder, no. 67b)

Marks: Struck on reverse with hallmarks (town mark, standard mark, date letter) and with maker's mark, one corner of the front of the rim struck with control mark O crowned

Description: Oblong, with incurved corners and slightly raised sides, on four angular bracket feet; the centre engraved with a coat of arms flanked by supporters and surmounted by a crown, all above foliate scroll mantling

H. 1¼ × W. 15¼ × D. 10¾ in. (3.1 × 38.7 × 27.3 cm)
Weight: 41 oz. (1277 g)

Heraldry: The arms are those of Willem IV, Prince of Orange-Nassau (1711–1751).

Provenance: Jonkheer J.W. van Vierssen Trip, 1941; Anonymous sale, Sotheby's, Amsterdam, June 2–3, 1992, lot 681

Published: Voet and van Gelder, p.167, no. 67b; Pijzel-Dommisse, p. 30

Jet Pijzel-Dommisse has noted that the same arms appear on a group of Hague silver dating from the 1720s which includes a wine cistern of 1720/21, mark of Jesias van Engauw, in the Rijksmuseum, Amsterdam, and two sugar casters of 1722/23 from the same workshop.

The son of Johan Willem Friso, Prince of Orange and head of the Friesian branch of the House of Orange-Nassau, Prince Willem was born just six weeks after his father's death in 1711. He succeeded his father as Stadtholder of Friesland and of Groningen, and in 1722, the year this salver was made, he was elected Stadtholder of Guelders. Although the prince was only 11 years of age, it is possible that this salver formed part of the plate acquired for this event. At the age of 23 he married Anne, the eldest daughter of George II of England. In 1747, with the French invasion, the States-General appointed him hereditary General Stadtholder of all seven Dutch provinces and he and his family moved from Leeuwarden to The Hague. He died in 1751.

47

The Domcha Collection

The salver illustrates the similarities between the utilitarian silver of northern European countries during the period. Dutch and English silver had enjoyed a long period of cross-fertilization, heightened by the accession of the Stadtholder Willem as King William III of England in 1688. Massive, plain silver in the French neo-classical taste became popular in England thanks to the influence of William's Dutch comrades who accompanied him to England. The Huguenot immigrants, many of whom came to London from France by way of the Low Countries, provided an experienced workforce to carry out commissions. In the 1720s, the arrival in The Hague of Lord Chesterfield's ambassadorial dinner service (see p. 50) in the French style similarly influenced local silversmiths.[1] Havelaar's mark is frequently found on salvers; interestingly, though, as in England, rectangular salvers are uncommon in Dutch silver.[2]

1. For example, Chesterfield's gilt sugar casters (see p. 50) were copied in The Hague by Christiaen Olislaegers in 1742 (Pijzel-Dommisse, p. 266, no. 86).
2. A similar example of oblong form, of 1727/28, was sold by Christie's, Amsterdam, December 12, 2006, lot 331.

48

Hot-milk jug

Silver (sterling standard), fruitwood

Dublin, 1724/25

Maker's mark: WB in script enclosed by a bell, possibly for William Barry

Marks: Struck under base with hallmarks (harp crowned, date letter) and with maker's mark; the cover flange with harp crowned and maker's mark

Description: Baluster, on spreading foot, with short spout, with teardrop at right angles to the wooden loop handle, the high hinged domed cover with baluster finial; the front engraved with a crest within a scroll and bellflower cartouche

H. 6¾ in. (17 cm)
Weight: 12 oz. 5 dwt. (380 g)

Heraldry: The crest pertains to a number of families.

This maker's mark appears in Jackson with an attribution to "William Bell". There does not, however, appear to be a William Bell recorded as a Dublin goldsmith, or as submitting plate for assay in Dublin. A more likely candidate is William Barry whose shop was at the Sign of the Bell in Skinner Row. He was admitted a free brother of the Dublin Goldsmiths' Company in 1709. He was elected Warden of the Company during the period 1715–1718 and served as Master in 1718–1719, 1719–1720 and 1733–1734. He was churchwarden of St Werburgh's in 1728 and was elected to the Common

48

48 crest

Geometry and the Silversmith

49

Council of the City of Dublin in 1732. Douglas Bennett attributes two marks, a *W.B in an oval* and a *WB in a rectangle*, to him.¹ In the surviving ledger of plate assayed during the period November 1, 1729–July 1733 Barry submitted 525 ounces for assay in 1729/30, 349 ounces in 1730/31, 157 in 1731/32 and 10 ounces for the period November–July 1733.²

1 Bennett, p. 139.
2 Sinsteden, "Assay Records 2", p. 97.

49

Teapot

Silver (sterling standard), fruitwood

London, 1724/25

Maker's mark: William Fawdery (Grimwade, no. 658)

Marks: Struck under base with hallmarks (lion passant, leopard's head and date letter) and with maker's mark, the interior of cover with maker's mark and lion passant

Description: Inverted pear shape on spreading foot, with octagonal tapering spout and octagonal handle sockets with wooden scroll handle, the flat hinged cover with wooden ball finial, the shoulder engraved with a band of trellis-work with bellflowers, scrolls and fish-scale at intervals; one side engraved with a coat of arms, crest and duke's coronet within a foliate scroll and trellis-work cartouche flanked by two eagles; engraved under the base with scratch weight *15"1* and with the initials *P over BB*

49 coat of arms

H. 5 × W. 9¼ × D. 4½ in. (12.7 × 23.5 × 11.4 cm)
Gross weight: 14 oz. 17 dwt. (463 g)

Heraldry: The arms are those of Bertie as borne by Peregrine, 2nd Duke of Ancaster (1686–1742).

Provenance: Peregrine, 2nd Duke of Ancaster (1686–1742)

Peregrine Bertie was the eldest son of Robert, 4th Earl of Lindsey who was created Duke of Ancaster in 1715 and died in 1723. Both father and son held the office of Lord Great Chamberlain and as such the 2nd Duke officiated at the coronation of George II. In 1711 he married Jane, third daughter of Sir John Brownlow, 3rd Bt. This teapot was presumably part of the plate ordered following his succession to the dukedom.

The Domcha Collection

50
Teapot

Silver (sterling standard)

London, 1725/26

Maker's mark: Simon Pantin I (Grimwade, no. 2606)

Description: Globular hexagonal on moulded hexagonal foot, with straight tapering spout and wooden loop handle, the shoulder engraved with a border of bellflowers; the flush hinged cover with wooden finial

H. 4¾ × W. 8½ × D. 4¼ (12.1 × 21.6 × 10.8 cm)
Gross weight: 13 oz. 10 dwt. (423 g)

Heraldry: The arms are those of Petty quartering those of FitzMaurice, as borne by Edmond, 1st Baron FitzMaurice (1846–1935).

Provenance: Edmond, 1st and last Baron FitzMaurice (1846–1935)

Hexagonal teapots are extremely rare.

51
Sugar bowl and cover

Silver (sterling standard)

London, 1725/26

Maker's mark: Benjamin Pyne (Grimwade, no. 3748)

Marks: Struck under base and on top of cover with hallmarks (lion passant, leopard's head, date letter) and with maker's mark

Description: Circular on spreading foot; the removable cover with rim foot; the side engraved with a coat of arms within a circular foliate scroll and fish-scale cartouche

H. 2⅞ × Diam. 3⅜ in. (7.4 × 8.6 cm)
Weight: 5 oz. 5 dwt. (162 g)

Heraldry: The arms are unidentified.

This unusually small sugar bowl and cover are from the workshop of Benjamin Pyne, whose mark appears on important silver from 1684 onwards. Pyne was one of the goldsmiths to the king, and was Prime Warden of the Goldsmiths' Company in 1725. However, in old age, he fell upon hard times and ended his life working as beadle (a form of doorman and messenger) of the Company.

52

Sugar bowl and cover

Silver (? sterling standard)

c.1720

Maker's mark: WN in script, probably for William Nicholson of Cork (Bowen and O'Brien, p. 34, no. CS11)

Marks: Struck under base and on top of cover with maker's mark

Description: Circular on reeded spreading foot, with reeded rim; the domed cover with similar rim and foot; the side engraved with a crest of a demi-lion; engraved under the base with scratch weight 7.2

H. 3¾ × Diam. 3⅞ in. (9.5 × 10 cm)
Weight: 6 oz. 12 dwt. (206 g)

Heraldry: The crest is one used by a number of families.

The mark *WN in script* had traditionally been ascribed to William Newenham of Cork, but in 2007 John Bowen and Conor O'Brien suggested a more likely candidate to be William Nicholson: "On the presumption that William Nicholson may have been an ancestor of the goldsmith John Nicholson, who sometimes used a mark JN in script, it is tentatively suggested that the script form of initials may have been a Nicholson family device".[1] William Nicholson is mentioned in documents in 1706 and 1714 and was admitted a freeman of the Cork Goldsmiths' Company in 1715.

1 Bowen and O'Brien, p. 34.

51, 52

The Domcha Collection

53

Coffee pot

Silver (sterling standard), fruitwood

London, 1728/29

Maker's mark: John Edwards II (Grimwade, no. 1267)

Marks: Struck on side with hallmarks (lion passant, leopard's head, date letter) and under base with maker's mark, the cover flange with lion passant

Description: Truncated octagonal pyramid on moulded foot, with octagonal swan-neck spout headed by stylized foliage and a vertical band and wooden scroll handle; the hinged domed cover with baluster finial; the side engraved with the royal arms within the Order of the Garter surmounted by a crown and flanked by the initials *GR*

H. 10 1/8 × W. 10 × D. 5 in. (25.6 × 25.5 × 12.7 cm)
Gross weight: 43 oz. 4 dwt. (1345 g)

Heraldry: The arms are, quarterly, those of 1, England impaling those of Scotland, 2, France, 3, Ireland and 4, Hanover, as borne by King George II (reigned 1727–1760).

The octagon became the most popular geometric shape for coffee and tea wares in the first decades of the eighteenth century. Proportionately, eight sides provide sufficiently wide surfaces for the addition of handle sockets, spouts and decorative armorials. As the opposing sides are parallel, it is also possible to place a spout either directly opposite a handle or at right angles to it. The first coffee pots had handles at right angles to the spout, but the more practical position opposite the spout was adopted during the first decade of the century. Thus less strain is put on the hand while pouring.

The proportions of the base to the height and the base to the width are almost exactly 1:2. The width from the outer edge of the handle to the tip of the spout thus forms a square with the height.

Plain geometric shapes such as this truncated octagonal pyramid could be made economically from sheet silver, beaten into the appropriate shape. This coffee pot is characterized by its extremely heavy gauge and the fine quality of its mouldings, neither of which is perhaps surprising given the presence of the royal arms on its side. Its octagonal form was, however, somewhat outmoded by the end of the 1720s, for most geometrically shaped pots date from the first and second decades of the century.

However, few coffee pots (as opposed to chocolate pots) appear before the reign of George II in the delivery books of the Jewel Office, the department of the Royal Household which distributed plate to ambassadors and other officials. One of the first of these was issued on February 15, 1727 to the Earl of Chesterfield:

One Coffee Pott and Saucer — 34 – 9 – 0[1]

This was part of a large delivery of gilt and white plate totalling nearly 6,000 ounces for Chesterfield to take on his embassy to The Hague. By the 1750s, a separate heading, "Coffee Room", appears in the delivery books, recording the movement of quantities of silver and gilt tea and coffee wares back and forth between the Jewel Office and the various royal residences.

The Jewel Office delivery and warrant books, now part of the Lord Chamberlain's records in the National Archives, do not, however, present the complete picture of all royal plate used in the early eighteenth century. It is evident that objects were purchased from silversmiths by members of the royal family and their households independently of the Jewel Office. It is therefore not surprising that this coffee pot does not appear in the records; nor do two important surviving silver-gilt tea services also engraved with the royal arms. The first, an extensive one which includes a coffee pot, is in a distinctive fluted form and dates from 1712/13 with the mark of Louis Mettayer;[2] the second is a silver-gilt tea service on tray, with baluster bodies, of 1721/22 with the mark of Philip Rollos II.[3]

John Edwards II, the son of an Oswestry innholder, was apprenticed to Thomas Pritchard in 1708 but he did not take up his freedom of the Goldsmiths' Company until 1723. As a journeyman he signed a petition against foreign workers who had not served a seven-year apprenticeship. His workshop in St Swithin's Lane was evidently a large one, and his output is of a consistently high standard. He made large-scale works, such as the large basket with lion handles of 1731/32 for the 8th Earl of Exeter,[4] several soup tureens with sculptural decoration, and a superb rococo inkstand of 1744/45, formerly in the Butlin Collection and now in a private South American collection.

Arthur Grimwade surmised that John Edwards II was the "Edwards" who was one of the Subordinate Goldsmiths to the King from 1723 to 1743.[5] This is confirmed by this coffee pot engraved with the royal arms, as well as by a sideboard dish delivered to Sir William Strickland in 1729 as a christening present for his son,[6] and other Edwards pieces engraved with the royal arms. Moreover, in October 1729, the delivery book of the Jewel Office lists, somewhat unusually, the names and in some cases includes the signatures of goldsmiths to whom items were sent for repair. Edwards was given "Six Acorn Sconces to mend & boyl", as well as a silver table (one of three sent out, and possibly one of the two surviving seventeenth-century silver tables in the Royal Collection), two stands or *guéridons* (which may also be one of the pairs remaining at Windsor) and an eight-branched chandelier. Against the entry is his signature.[7]

1 NA [PRO]/LC/9/44, f. 297.
2 Probably originally belonging to Ralph Montagu and now in the Buccleuch Collection at Boughton House, Northamptonshire; see Glanville, "Boughton", p. 154, plate 89.

Geometry and the Silversmith

53

54

3 Sold Sotheby's, London, April 8, 1954, lot 136, subsequently in the collection of Nathaniel, 3rd Baron Rothschild.
4 Formerly in the collection of Mrs. Walter M. Jeffords and offered Sotheby's, New York, October 26, 2005, lot 303.
5 Grimwade, p. 501.
6 Sold Sotheby's, London, June 27, 1963, lot 35.
7 NA [PRO]/LC/9/44, f. 311.

54

Two-handled bowl

Silver (sterling standard)

Newcastle, 1728/29

Maker's mark: Thomas Partis I of Sunderland and Durham (Gill, p. 182)

Marks: Struck under base with hallmarks (three-tower mark, lion passant, leopard's head, date letter) and with trace of the maker's mark, the two handles with maker's mark

Description: Circular with everted sides and moulded rim, on spreading foot, with two tubular scroll handles with triangular terminals; the front engraved with a coat of arms within an architectural scroll and rusticated cartouche surmounted by a shell and flanked by mermaids, with a devil's mask below

H. 7¾ × W. 17½ × D. 11¾ in. (18.7 × 44.4 × 29.8 cm)
Weight: 89 oz. 10 dwt. (2785 g)

Heraldry: The arms are those of Ashburnham.

Provenance: R.L. Petterson, Esq., Sotheby's, London, February 2, 1961, lot 111

Published: Holland, illustrated p. 208

The large and shallow proportions of this bowl suggest that it was intended for punch.

Thomas Partis I was a silversmith in the High Street, Sunderland, who later moved to Durham. In 1720, he ran foul of the Newcastle Goldsmiths' Company for "exerciseing the business of a Goldsmith having not served his time to a Goldsmith & neglecting to get his plate Essayed". Partis duly paid his dues to the Company and, as this cup shows, he sent his silver to the Newcastle assay office for marking. His workshop made a number of large-scale pieces and the *Newcastle Courant* for October 18, 1740 recorded: "Yesterday was assay'd at the Assay office in this Town, a Piece of Plate made by Mr Partis, of the City of Durham; and that the same having been view'd by some of the best judges, it was allow'd to be a most curious and valuable Piece of Workmanship, especially being done by one Hand". A few years later, however, tragedy struck. The *Newcastle Journal* for December 5, 1747 reported that "On Friday 7 night, in the Evening, Mr Thomas Partis, a Silversmith, late of Sunderland, was found dead in the Road near Keswick in Cumberland, supposed to be robb'd and murder'd. Two old Men who first saw him in that Condition went to a House to call Assistance, and on their Return he was found stript stark naked; so that 'tis supposed the Rogues were near. The Coroner's Jury sat on the Body, and brought in their Verdict Wilful Murder".

55, 56

55

Coffee pot

Silver (sterling standard), fruitwood

London, 1728/29

Maker's mark: John White (Grimwade, no. 1735)

Marks: Struck on rim with hallmarks (lion passant, leopard's head, date letter), interior of cover with lion passant, under base with maker's mark

Description: Of small size, truncated conical on moulded foot, straight octagonal tapering spout and wooden loop handle; the low domed hinged cover with air hole and vase-shaped finial; the side engraved with a coat of arms flanked by supporters with a ribbon motto below and a baron's coronet above

H. 6 × W. 6½ × D. 3⅜ (15.2 × 16.5 × 8.6 cm)
Gross weight: 13 oz. 10 dwt. (421 g)

Heraldry: The arms are those King impaling those of Seys, as borne by Peter King, 1st Baron King (1669–1734).

Provenance: Peter King, 1st Baron King (1669–1734), by descent to Manon, Countess of Lovelace, The Executry [sic] of Manon, Countess of Lovelace, sale, Christie's, London, May 12, 1993, lot 144

Peter King studied at the University of Leiden and was called to the Bar in 1698. He entered Parliament as a Whig in 1701. In 1714, as Recorder of London, he greeted George I with the Mayor and Corporation of London as the new king entered the city. His loyalty to the new dynasty greatly helped both his legal and his political career. In 1725, he succeeded Lord Macclesfield as Speaker of the House of Lords, following the latter's impeachment for corruption. Shortly afterwards, he was created Baron King of Ockham and appointed Lord Chancellor. A cultured man, he published books on theology, was a member of the Royal Society and a friend of Sir Isaac Newton. His mother was first cousin of John Locke. His house, Ockham Park, was remodelled by Nicholas Hawksmoor between 1725 and 1729. Lord King's most valuable contribution to English politics was the Act that put an end to the fraudulent sale of offices.

King and his successors were considerable patrons of the goldsmith John White between 1728 and 1737. White is a

55 achievement

somewhat shadowy figure who may have been a retailer rather than a manufacturing silversmith. Much of the silver bearing his mark is identical to works from Paul de Lamerie's workshop.[1]

[1] A large part of the King family's silver was sold in two auctions in the 1990s: the 1993 sale cited above and another, Sotheby's, London, June 8, 1995. For a John White cup and cover, made for John, 2nd Lord King, see Hartop, *Huguenot*, p. 116, no. 12.

56
Coffee pot

Silver (sterling standard), fruitwood

London, 1724/25

Maker's mark: Thomas Tearle (Grimwade, no. 2938)

Marks: Struck on rim with hallmarks (lion passant, leopard's head, date letter) and with maker's mark, the interior of the cover with lion passant

Description: Of small size, truncated conical on spreading foot, with straight tapering spout and wooden scroll handle at right angles; the high-domed cover with ball finial; the front engraved with a lozenge of arms suspended from a ribbon

H. 6⅛ × W. 5⅞ × D. 4½ in. (15.5 × 15 × 11.5 cm)
Gross weight: 10 oz. (309 g)

Heraldry: The arms, which are depicted in a lozenge to denote a lady, are impossible to identify as the colours are not delineated: "A chevron between three leopards' heads" pertains to many families.

Thomas Tearle was apprenticed to Gabriel Sleath in 1707 and registered his mark as a largeworker in 1719. Grimwade observes: "As one would expect from his apprenticeship, Tearle is an excellent general maker of cups, tankards and salvers, without ever aspiring to important pieces, or displaying great originality."[1]

[1] Grimwade, p. 679.

57
Waiter

Silver (sterling standard)

London, 1729/30

Maker's mark: Matthew Cooper I (Grimwade, no. 2003)

Marks: Struck on reverse with hallmarks (lion passant, leopard's head, date letter) and with maker's mark

Description: Square with incurved corners and moulded rim, raised on four shaped bracket feet; the reverse with scratch weight *8 oz. 8*.

H. ¾ × W. 5¼ × D. 5¼ in. (1.7 × 13.3 × 13.3 cm)
Weight: 8 oz. 5 dwt. (259 g)

For information about square and oblong salvers, see no. 46.

58
Pair of mugs

Silver (sterling standard)

London, 1729/30

Maker's mark: Francis Nelme (Grimwade, no. 67)

Marks: One struck under base with hallmarks (lion passant, leopard's head and date letter) and with maker's mark; the other with maker's mark struck four times

Description: Baluster on spreading foot, with scroll handles, the fronts engraved with a coat of arms and crest within a foliate scroll and trellis-work cartouche with a human mask below

H. 3¾ × W. 4½ × D. 3⅛ in. (9.5 × 11.4 × 7.9 cm)
Weight: 17 oz. 10 dwt. (544 g)

Heraldry: The arms are those of Addington impaling those of another.

Provenance: H.R. Creswick, sale, Sotheby's, London, November 30, 1972, lot 111; anonymous sale, Sotheby's, New York, April 22, 1998, lot 273

Published: Brett, p. 193, no. 812

58

59

Chocolate pot

Silver (sterling standard), fruitwood

Dublin, 1729/30, or possibly 1694/95

Maker's mark: Caleb Rotheram of Cork (Bowen and O'Brien, p. 185, column 2, line 2)

Marks: Struck under base and on interior of cover with hallmarks (harp crowned, date letter) and with maker's mark under base

Description: Truncated conical on moulded foot, with tapering swan-neck spout and wooden loop handle issuing from wavy cut-card cartouches and scalloped sockets at right angles to the spout; the hinged domed cover with fluted scroll thumbpiece and central sliding cap enclosed by cut card, with acorn finial; the front engraved with a coat of arms and crest within foliate scroll mantling; engraved under the base with initials *EB* over *V* over *RE* flanked by *1701*

H. $8^{3}/_{4}$ × W. 7 × D. $6^{7}/_{8}$ in. (22 × 17.8 × 17.5 cm)
Gross weight: 28 oz. 5 dwt. (874 g)

Heraldry: The arms are those of Gordon quartering those of probably Preston.

Provenance: Viscount Rochdale, removed from Lingholm, Cumbria, sale, Sotheby's, West Wycombe Park, June 22, 1998, lot 503

This pot is struck with the mark of a Cork goldsmith but also bears Dublin hallmarks. It presents an intriguing problem in dating. When sold at auction

59

The Domcha Collection

in 1998 it was dated 1694/95. At the end of the seventeenth century the Dublin Goldsmiths' Company used two punches, the harp crowned and a date letter. However, an identical harp crowned and date letter were also used for both that year and 1729/30. Stylistically, this pot could be as early as 1694/95, and certainly a handful of Irish chocolate pots from before 1700 is known.[1]

Caleb Rotheram was one of the leading goldsmiths working in Cork at the beginning of the eighteenth century. Although he is not recorded as receiving his freedom until 1701, it is also possible he was working as early as 1694/95. He served as Warden of the Cork Goldsmiths' Company in 1702 and was Master of the Company in 1707.[2] He died in 1746.

A look at the relations between the Cork goldsmiths and the Dublin Goldsmiths' Company suggests, however, that a date of 1729/30 for the pot is more likely. During the second half of the seventeenth century, and into the second decade of the eighteenth, a town mark of a ship was used in Cork. Thomas Sinsteden has written: "The Cork goldsmiths ceased to use the town mark in the late Queen Anne period and at the same time began to send at least a portion of their wrought silver in packages to Dublin for hallmarking. It is most probable that Cork complied to a directive from the [Company of Goldsmiths of Dublin]."[3] An analysis by Dr Sinsteden of silver by Cork makers hallmarked in Dublin during the first half of the eighteenth century shows that the quantity peaked in the years 1725–8. The same maker's mark and Dublin harp and date letter appear on a single-handled porringer in the National Museum of Ireland.

1. A similar example to this pot is one marked Dublin, 1693/94, mark of John Humphreys, advertised by Spink and Son Ltd. in *Apollo*, September 1974. Another Dublin example of 1696/97, mark of Thomas Bolton, is in the National Museum, Dublin (Teahan, p. 13, no. 8).
2. Bennett, p. 186; Bowen and O'Brien, p. 185.
3. Thomas Sinsteden, "A 'sterling' relationship: the Cork goldsmiths and the Company of Goldsmiths of Dublin", in Bowen and O'Brien, p. 20, and Sinsteden, "Assay Records 2", p. 91.

60

Pair of fluted dishes

Silver (sterling standard)

London, 1729/30

Maker's mark: David Willaume II (Grimwade, no. 514)

Marks: Struck reverses with hallmarks (lion passant, leopard's head and date letter) and with maker's mark

Description: Circular, with deep sides with twenty radiating flutes and scalloped rims; the centres engraved with a coat of arms within the Order of the Garter, surmounted by a duke's coronet and flanked by supporters, with a foliate scroll and scalework plinth and motto below, the reverses engraved, probably in the nineteenth century, with a crest and baron's coronet

H. 1⅞ × Diam. 9¼ in. (5 × 23.5 cm)
Weight: 43 oz. 10 dwt. (1351 g)

Heraldry: The arms are those of Pelham, as borne by Thomas Pelham, later Pelham-Holles, 1st Duke of Newcastle-upon-Tyne (1693–1768). The later crest on the reverses is that of Bass, as borne by Michael, Baron Burton (1837–1909), chairman of the brewery Bass and Company of Burton-on-Trent.

Provenance: Thomas Pelham, later Pelham-Holles, 1st Duke of Newcastle-upon-Tyne (1693–1768); Michael, 1st Baron Burton (1837–1909); Sotheby's, London, March 1, 1962, lot 131; Neville Hamwee, sale, Sotheby's, London, May 30, 1963, lot 18

David Willaume II was apprenticed to his father, also David, a Huguenot immigrant from Metz who traded as a goldsmith and also kept "running cashes" (i.e. a bank) in St James's. The Willaume workshop produced some of the most ambitious plate of the first quarter of the eighteenth century. At the age of 16, David II was sent by his father to France to claim his inheritance. He attained his Freedom of the Goldsmiths' Company in 1723 but did not enter his own mark until his father retired about 1728 and he took over the workshop. These dishes are therefore among his first works. For fluted dishes made for the same patron by his father, see no. 38.

Circular fluted dishes are usually described as "sallet dishes" in eighteenth century bills and inventories, sallet referring to cooked, as well as raw, vegetables. They formed part of the service for the first two courses, or removes, of a dinner and would have been placed on the table between

59 coat of arms

Geometry and the Silversmith

60

Thomas Pelham, later Pelham-Holles, 1st Duke of Newcastle-upon-Tyne (1693–1768) by William Hoare, pastel. *National Portrait Gallery, London*

elliptical or oblong platters with meat, fowl or fish on them. Fluted dishes first appear about 1700 and were clearly based on Asian ceramic prototypes, which in turn were probably inspired by carved jade and bronze examples. The term "strawberry dish" given to fluted dishes in the nineteenth century was no doubt thought to make them more attractive to potential buyers after the demise of *service à la française*.

Thomas Pelham, nephew of John, 1st Duke of Newcastle-upon-Tyne of the second creation, was born in 1693. A Whig and zealous supporters of the Hanoverians, he enjoyed rapid advancement, first in the Royal Household and then in cabinet government, culminating in his appointment as First Lord of the Treasury, or Prime Minister, in 1754. He led the government for eighteen months and then again from July 1757 to May 1762. Lord Chesterfield made this observation on his life and career: "He was good-natured, to a degree of weakness, even to tears, upon the slightest occasion. Exceedingly timorous, both personally and politically … His ruling, or rather his only, passion was the agitation, the bustle, and the hurry of business … but he was as dilatory in dispatching it as he was eager to engage in it … Upon the whole, he was a compound of most human weaknesses, but untainted by any vice or crime … He retired from business in the year 1762, above four hundred thousand pounds poorer than when he first engaged in it."[1] Pelham had been created 1st Duke of Newcastle-upon-Tyne of the third creation in

77

61, 62

1715.[2] He married in 1717 Henrietta, eldest daughter and co-heiress of Francis, 2nd Earl of Godolphin. The marriage produced no heirs and in 1756 he was given a new dukedom, that of Newcastle-under-Line with a special remainder to his cousin and heir, Thomas Pelham of Stanmer.[3]

1 Quoted in *Complete Peerage, sub* Newcastle.
2 His uncle John, 1st Duke of Newcastle-upon-Tyne of the second creation, had died in 1711, when all his titles became extinct.
3 Spelt *Line* in the patent of creation, not *Lyme*.

61

Sugar box or bowl and cover

Silver (? sterling standard)

c.1730

Maker's mark: Unknown

Marks: None

Description: Elliptical baluster on spreading foot, the domed cover with moulded rim and elliptical vase-shaped finial; the side and cover engraved with a crest; engraved under the base with scratch weight *13=8*

H. 4¾ × W. 4¼ × D. 3¼ in. (12 × 10.6 × 8.2 cm)
Weight: 13 oz. 3 dwt. (409 g)

Heraldry: The crest, that of a stag's head, pertains to many families.

This bowl has no marks. Judging from its quality and the use of cast components it is unlikely to be a provincial piece. The law stated that objects that were offered for sale had to be assayed and hallmarked. If an object was commissioned and the silver for it supplied by old, outmoded, pieces that were effectively converted into the new object, it could be argued that the object was not being "set for sale" and therefore did not require hallmarking. This became a much more attractive option after 1719 with the introduction of duty on wrought plate of 6d per ounce.

Most sugar boxes of the first half of the eighteenth century are rectangular or polygonal. This elliptical baluster example is unusual and should be compared with the 2nd Earl of Warrington's "Two gilt Sugar Boxes with Covers" of 1730/31, mark of John Liger, at Dunham Massey.[1]

1 Lomax and Rothwell, p. 86, no. 33.

62

Cream jug

Silver (Britannia standard)

London, 1720/21

Maker's mark: Samuel Wastell (Grimwade, no. 2991)

Marks: Struck with hallmarks (Britannia, lion's head, date letter) and with maker's mark

Description: Baluster on moulded foot, ruled rim, with short spout and scroll handle; the side engraved with a mirrored cipher within a circular foliate scroll cartouche

H. 3⅝ × W. 3⅝ × D. 2¾ in. (9 × 9 × 7 cm)
Weight: 6 oz. 5 dwt. (195 g)

For details about Samuel Wastell, see no. 29.

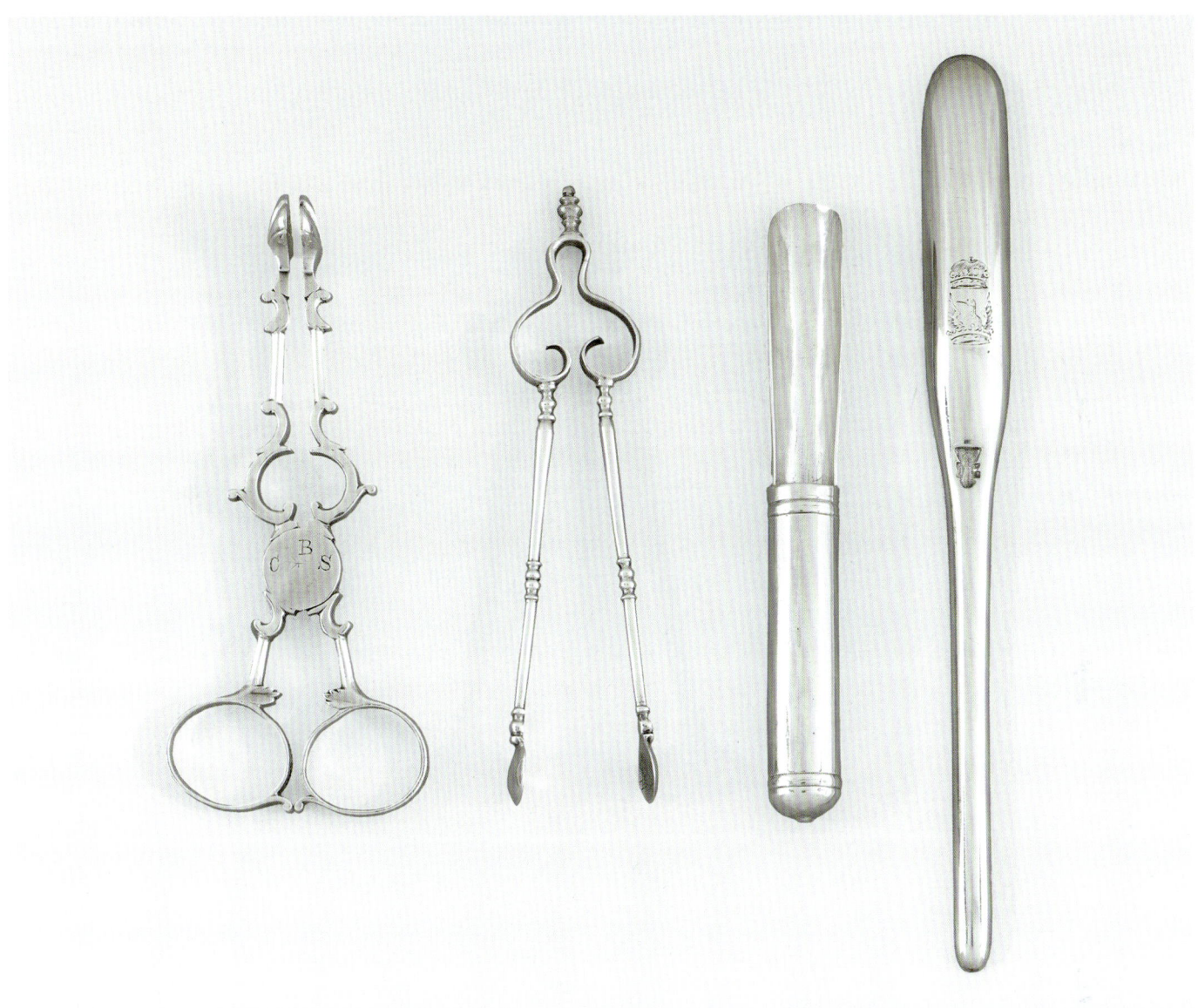

63, 64, 65, 66

63

Sugar tongs

Silver (sterling standard)

London, c. 1730

Maker's mark: HP, probably for Humphrey Phillips (cf. Grimwade, no. 1057)

Marks: Struck on finger holes with hallmark (lion passant) and maker's mark

Description: Scissor form, with multi-scroll arms and shell grips; engraved with the initials *B* over *CS*

H. 5/8 × W. 4 3/4 × D. 2 in. (2.4 × 12 × 5 cm)
Weight: 1 oz. 4 dwt. (37 g)

The scissor-form sugar tongs replaced the fire-tong type (see no. 64) in the 1730s.

64

Sugar tongs

Silver (Britannia standard)

London, c. 1715

Maker's mark: Thomas Stackhouse (Grimwade, no. 2639)

Marks: Struck on one grip with hallmark (lion's head) and on the other with maker's mark

Description: In the form of miniature fire tongs, with baluster stems and finials, and elliptical grips

H. 5/8 × W. 4 3/4 × D. 1 1/4 in. (1.2 × 12 × 3.2 cm)
Weight: 10 dwt. (15 g)

Sugar was chipped off a sugarloaf in the shape of a cone and introduced to the tea table in a sugar bowl, with or without a cover. Elegant tongs following the form of fire tongs were made from the second decade of the eighteenth century until replaced with the more common scissor variety (see no. 63) in the 1730s.

79

The Domcha Collection

65

Apple corer

Silver (? sterling standard)

c. 1690

Maker's mark: Unknown

Marks: None

Description: Cylindrical with cannon end, engraved with reeding and the initials A Y

H. ½ × W. 4¾ × D. ½ in. (1.25 × 12.1 × 1.25 cm)
Weight: 12 dwt. (20 g)

Provenance: The Albert Collection

Published: Butler, *Albert*, p. 140, no. 135

An apple corer was an essential component of a traveller's kit and is often found as part of a compendium of eating implements in a fitted case. This corer is among the earliest recorded. The small size is explained by the fact that modern apples have been bred to be much larger than early varieties.

66

Marrow spoon

Silver (? sterling standard)

c. 1710

Maker's mark: Pierre Platel of London (Grimwade, no. 2200)

Marks: Struck on reverse with maker's mark

Description: Double-ended, the back engraved with a crest under a baron's coronet

H. ¼ × W. 7 × D. ¾ in. (0.6 × 17.8 × 1.8 cm)
Weight: 1 oz. 10 dwt. (47 g)

Heraldry: The crest and coronet are those of Hutchinson, Baron Donoughmore.

The *London Gazette* in 1693 refers to "marrow-spoons", by which name these implements were known until the nineteenth century when the term marrow scoop first appears.

67

Cake basket

Silver (sterling standard)

London, 1731/32

Maker's mark: Paul Crespin (Grimwade, no. 2143a)

Marks: Struck under base with hallmarks (lion passant, leopard's head, date letter) and with maker's mark

Description: Elliptical, the everted sides pierced with trellis-work within a scalloped rim applied with gadrooning, with overhead swing handle applied with twisted wire; the centre engraved with a coat of arms within an asymmetrical foliate scroll, flower and *rocaille* cartouche; engraved under the base with scratch weight *63=15*

H. 11¾ × W. 13⅜ × D. 11¼ in. (29.8 × 34 × 28.6 cm)
Weight: 60 oz. 15 dwt. (1891 g)

Heraldry: The arms are those of Fountayne impaling those of Bromley, as borne by John Fountayne (1715–1802).

Provenance: John Fountayne, DD (1715–1802)

A similar basket with the mark of Crespin, of 1734/35, is in the collection of Gonville and Caius College, Cambridge. In his long working career Paul Crespin produced some of the most cosmopolitan silver of the period. He was part of the "Lamerie group" of suppliers, most of them, like him, Huguenots, who exchanged patterns and finished work. Crespin's mark appears on some objects overstruck by Paul de Lamerie and it may be that he was a manufacturing silversmith rather than a retail supplier, although in 1724 he showed "a fine silver bathing vessel (made for the King of Portugal) to his Majesty at Kensington who was well pleased with so curious a piece of workmanship".[1]

John Fountayne DD, Dean of York, married, as his first wife, Anne, daughter of William Bromley, Speaker of the House of Commons and Secretary of State under Queen Anne. Fountayne succeeded to the estates of his brother Thomas Fountayne of Melton, Yorkshire, in 1739 and died in 1802.

1 Murdoch, "Harpies", p. 456.

68

Pair of sauce-boats

Silver (sterling standard)

London, 1731/32

Maker's mark: Anne Tanqueray (Grimwade, no. 100)

Marks: Struck under base with hallmarks (lion passant, leopard's head, date letter) and with maker's mark

Description: Elliptical double-lipped on spreading elliptical foot, shaped moulded rims, each with two scroll handles set along the

68

long sides; the sides engraved with a coat of arms within a foliate scroll and fish-scale cartouche

H. 4³⁄₈ × W. 8¹⁄₈ × D. 7¹⁄₂ in. (11 × 20.5 × 19 cm)
Weight: 34 oz. 4 dwt. (1064 g)

Heraldry: The arms are those of Bullen impaling those of Aston of Devon.

Provenance: Property of a Gentleman, sale, Christie's, London, March 10, 1920, lot 112; anonymous sale, Christie's, London, November 17, 1964, lot 176; The Palladio Stiftung, Liechtenstein, sale, Christie's, London, June 26, 1974, lot 112; A New York Collector, sale, Christie's, New York, April 18, 1989, lot 515

Exhibited: Cambridge, Fitzwilliam Museum, March 15, 1969– March 15, 1970

These sauce-boats follow a model first produced in France at the beginning of the eighteenth century. The French fashion for sauces became widespread on fashionable English tables during the first decades of the century.

Anne Tanqueray was part of a close-knit group of Huguenot families who were central to the silversmiths' trade in the first half of the eighteenth century. The eldest daughter of David Willaume I, the goldsmith banker of St James's (see p. 76), she married another Huguenot goldsmith, David Tanqueray, in 1717, who had been apprenticed to her father in 1708. Tanqueray had registered his own mark in 1713 and by 1720 was established in fashionable Pall Mall. The couple had two sons, both of whom entered the church, one of them as rector of Tingrith in Bedfordshire, where his grandfather Willaume had purchased an estate and where he retired around 1728. Some time after 1724 David Tanqueray died, although his exact date of death is unknown, and Anne as his widow continued to run the business, as often happened when there was no son old enough to take it over. She registered two new marks at Goldsmiths' Hall, but instead of creating a new entry for her in the record book, the clerk entered them against her husband's entry of 1713 and replaced his name with hers. David Tanqueray is recorded as one of the Subordinate Goldsmiths to the King in 1729 and 1732 but, as Arthur Grimwade surmises, it is most likely he was already dead by then and Anne was in charge of the business in a managerial capacity rather than as a practising silversmith. Grimwade notes that "the quality of her sauce-boats and inkstands is particularly outstanding".[1] She died in 1733. A similar pair of sauce-boats from the Tanqueray workshops, hallmarked 1727/28, was sold from the collection of Mrs C.J. Devine, Christie's, London, October 15, 1985, lot 1204.

1 Grimwade, p. 676.

69

Wine-bottle stand

Silver (sterling standard)

London, 1733/34

Maker's mark: John Gamon (Grimwade, no. 1323)

Marks: Struck under base with hallmarks (lion passant, leopard's head, date letter) and with maker's mark

Description: Elliptical with moulded rim, on spreading foot; the side engraved with a crest; fitted with a nineteenth-century green glass bottle

H. 2⁵⁄₈ × W. 4¹⁄₄ × D. 3⁷⁄₈ in. (6.5 × 10.8 × 9.8 cm)
Weight of silver: 5 oz. 12 dwt. (176 g)

Heraldry: The crest pertains to several families.

The development of the glass wine bottle, thanks to Huguenot immigrant glass blowers at the end of the seventeenth century, meant that wine could be kept for much longer in the cellar. The earliest bottles often had a rounded body which would not stand up, making a stand such as this example necessary.

This stand appears to be a smaller version of what the Jewel Office delivery book 44 records as "Two flask Stands" weighing some 39 ounces, delivered to the Speaker of the Commons, Arthur Onslow, on March 9, 1727.[1] An example of 1723/24 with the mark of Augustine Courtauld, weighing some 19 ounces, is in the Farrer Collection in the Ashmolean Museum, Oxford,[2] one of 1715/16, mark of Anthony Nelme, weighing 18 ounces was sold in 1981,[3] and another weighing 6 ounces 8 pennyweights, of 1716/17 with the mark of Simon Pantin, was formerly in the Albert Collection.[4]

1 NA [PRO] LC/9/44 f. 300.
2 Jones, *Farrer*, p. 110, plate LVII.
3 Sotheby's, London, August 23, 1981, lot 220.
4 Sold by Christie's, London, June 15, 1983, lot 191, illustrated in Clayton, *History*, p. 113, no. 14 and in Butler, *Albert*, p. 264, no. 110.

68 coat of arms

Geometry and the Silversmith

69, 70

70

Funnel

Silver (Britannia standard)

London, 1717/18

Maker's mark: Simon Pantin I (Grimwade, no. 2125)

Marks: Struck on side with hallmarks (Britannia, lion's head, date letter) and with maker's mark

Description: Conical with moulded rim; the side engraved with a crest

H. 4 × Diam. 3⅛ in. (10.1 × 8 cm)
Weight: 3 oz. (98 g)

Heraldry: The crest is unidentified.

The Domcha Collection

71

72

84

71

Pair of beakers

Silver (sterling standard)

London, 1735/36

Maker's mark: Edward Pocock (Grimwade, no. 632)

Marks: Struck under bases with hallmarks (lion passant, leopard's head and date letter) and with maker's mark

Description: With slightly everted sides, on moulded bases

H. 4½ × Diam. 3¾ in. (11.4 × 9.5 cm)

Weight: 20 oz. 15 dwt. (645 g)

Provenance: Anonymous sale, Sotheby's, London, November 29, 2005, lot 158

Edward Pocock was apprenticed to John Wisdome, goldsmith, who was a freeman of the Haberdashers' Company. In London it was necessary to be a member of a livery company in order to be a freeman of the city and practise a trade within it, but it was not necessary to belong to the company concerned with your trade. The apprenticeship and freedom records for both Wisdome and Pocock appear in the Haberdashers' Company archives, not the Goldsmiths'. Pocock entered his first mark as a largeworker in partnership with Hugh Arnett, in 1720, giving an address in Foster Lane.

72

Salver

Silver (sterling standard)

London, 1736/37

Maker's mark: Edward Feline (Grimwade, no. 576)

Marks: Struck on reverse with hallmarks (lion passant, leopard's head, date letter) and with maker's mark

Description: Rectangular with incurved corners and raised sides, on four shaped bracket-scroll feet

H. 1¼ × W. 8¾ × D. 6 in. (3.1 × 22.2 × 15.2 cm)

Weight: 11 oz. (345 g)

Edward Feline was apprenticed to Augustine Courtauld in 1709 and was admitted a freeman in 1721. His son, also Edward, was apprenticed to him in 1745. Feline was dead by 1753, when his widow Magdalen entered a mark, presumably because his son by that time was working in the Assay Office at Goldsmiths' Hall.

73

Dish

Silver (sterling standard)

London, 1737/38

Maker's mark: Paul de Lamerie (Hare, no. 4)

Marks: Struck on reverse with hallmarks (lion passant, leopard's head, date letter) and with maker's mark

Description: Plain circular with moulded rim and central well; the border engraved with a coat of arms within a foliate scroll and rusticated cartouche and, opposite, with a crest and an earl's coronet; the reverse engraved *No. 3* and with scratch weight *36=11*

H. 1 × Diam. 12 in. (2.5 × 30.6 cm)

Weight: 32 oz. 10 dwt. (1015 g)

Heraldry: The arms are those of Mildmay quartering those of Fitzwalter with those of Schomberg on an escutcheon of pretence, as borne by Benjamin Mildmay, 19th Baron Fitzwalter (1672–1756), created Earl Fitzwalter in 1735.

Provenance: Benjamin Mildmay, 1st Earl Fitzwalter (1672–1756); subsequent history unknown until anonymous sale, Sotheby Parke Bernet, New York, October 26–27, 1976, lot 406; Francis E. Fowler III, sale, Sotheby's, New York, October 21, 1998, lot 87

Benjamin Mildmay was the younger son of an Essex landowner who, in 1670, had successfully claimed the ancient barony of Fitzwalter which had fallen into abeyance in 1648. As A. C. Edwards observed, for the first fifty years of his life Mildmay "rested in the quasi-obscurity appropriate to a younger son". He was equerry to Queen Anne's consort, Prince George of Denmark, and was Chief Commissioner of the Salt Duties, 1714–1720, and served as Commissioner of Excise, 1720–1728.

Then, in 1724 at the age of fifty-one, Mildmay fell in love with and married Frederica Darcy, the daughter of

73 coat of arms

73

Meinhardt, Duke of Schomberg, and granddaughter of the great military commander, Marshall Schomberg. Frederica was also a kinswoman of the royal family, for she was granddaughter of Charles Louis, Elector Palatine who was uncle of George I. A widow, she had had two children by her marriage to Lord Holderness. Lady Mary Wortley Montagu observed that the love between Mildmay and Lady Holderness was "as curious as between two oysters",[1] but despite their difference in age they appear to have lived happily together for twenty-seven years. In 1728, on the death of his brother, Mildmay became Lord Fitzwalter and succeeded to his family's estates. At once he began to remodel Moulsham Hall in Essex with the help of the Italian architect Giacomo Leoni, while in London he and his wife lived in great state at Schomberg House, the Duke of Schomberg's town house in Pall Mall. With his new wife's connections, he rapidly advanced at court, being created Earl Fitzwalter in 1730. One of the group of Whigs who maintained a distance from Walpole (see the note about William Duff, no. 36), he became Chief Commissioner of the Board of Trade and Plantations in 1735 and Treasurer of the Household in 1737.

Lord Fitzwalter's life would not be of much interest were it not for the meticulous account books he kept for virtually all of his married life, itemizing his income and expenditure in great detail, interspersed with comments on the news of the day. Silver purchases from some six goldsmiths, including John

An Account of the Right Hon:ble the Earl of
Fitzwalter's Plate taken this 22 day of June 1739.
Viz:

		ounces
1 Large Soup Dish weighing		77 : 10 : —
1 Oval Dish Do		92 : 3 : —
1 Round Dish No: 1		60 : 13 : —
No 1 — 1 Do No Do		61 : 0 : —
1 Do No Do		61 : 0 : —
1 Do No 2		46 : 3
1 Do No 2		52 : 7
No 2 — 1 Do No Do		45 : —
1 Do No Do		45 : —
1 Do No 3		39 : 10 : —
1 Do No Do		42 : 14 : —
1 Do No Do		36 : 7 : —
No 3 — 1 Do No Do		40 : 0 : —
1 Do No Do		36 : 11 : —
1 Do No Do		40 : 4 : —
1 Do No Do		40 : 0 : —
1 Do No Do		40 : 15 : —
1 Do No 4		31 : 14 : —
1 Do No Do		33 : 4 : —
No 4 — 1 Do No Do		29 : 4 : —
1 Do No Do		32 : 5 : —
1 Do No Do		31 : 18 : —
5 Dozen of plates: all Number'd		1229 : 2 : —
1 Large Oval Terreen & Cover		204 : 0 : —
1 Round Terreen & Cover		155 : 4 : —
1 Do & Cover		156 : 12 : —
1 Large Tea Table		150 : 0 : —
An Epargne being 2 Rings, 4 buttons, 4 Saucers, 1 Round Bason, 4 Branches, 1 Sivett & lamp		202 : 8 : —
Carried forward		

Inventory of Lord Fitzwalter's plate made on June 22, 1739. *Essex Record Office, Chelmsford*

The Domcha Collection

White and Henry Hebert, are included, but it is his account with Paul de Lamerie, extending over ten years and one of the handful of surviving accounts from this important workshop, which provides a mass of detail of great importance to silver historians. Three of Lamerie's bills out of a total of four appear to have survived, presented to Fitzwalter between about 1725 and 1738; the accounts overlap and it is clear that Fitzwalter, like so many of his contemporaries, was dilatory in paying.[2]

This dish is part of an extensive dinner service listed in the accounts, bought from Lamerie in two waves, in 1727–28 and 1737–38.[3] Three dozen plates and a dozen dishes, all with plain moulded borders, appear to have been purchased in the first instalment, with additional dishes, including the present example, added some ten years later. For the fashionable *service à la française*, it was necessary to have several dozen serving dishes and at least three dozen dinner plates.

On his appointment as Treasurer of the Household in 1737, Fitzwalter also received an allowance of plate from the Jewel Office including a further dozen dinner plates, although it is interesting to note that these were evidently standard Royal Household issue and had gadrooned, rather than moulded, borders.[4] The page of the delivery book lists the pieces together with the signatures of William Wilkins, the earl's valet, who signed that he had "Recefd by his horder" four candlesticks, and of Henry Longmore, the earl's butler.

Wilkins and Longmore were also signatories to an inventory made of all the earl's plate on June 22, 1739 by Henry Hebert,[5] who figures elsewhere in the Fitzwalter accounts described as "silversmith and excise man". Besides the extensive service of plates and dishes, the inventory includes tureens, candlesticks and tea and coffee wares totalling some 4,684 ounces. The larger circular dishes in the service, of which this dish is one, appear not to have been numbered consecutively but grouped by sizes: this twelve-inch example is one of the eight in group 3.

1   Quoted in *Complete* Peerage, *sub* Fitzwalter.
2   Essex Record Office, Chelmsford, Mildmay Accounts, D/DM/A6. Five account books are in the Essex Record Office; another is in the Dogmersfield archives in the Hampshire Record Office. A seventh appears to be missing. For an excellent discussion of the earl and his accounts, see A.C. Edwards, *The Account Books of Benjamin Mildmay, Earl Fitzwalter*, London, 1977.
3   Most of the plates and dishes survive in museums and collections, the largest part being in the Sterling and Francine Clark Art Institute in Williamstown, Massachusetts. See Wees, pp. 152–3, where a comprehensive list of auction appearances of the components of the service is given, and Hartop, *Huguenot*, pp. 110–15, for a discussion of other pieces in the service.
4   NA [PRO]/ LC/9/45 f.63.
5   Essex Record Office, Chelmsford, Mildmay Accounts, D/DM/F12.

74

Wine siphon

Silver (? sterling standard), cork

c. 1740

Maker's mark: John Harvey I of London (Grimwade, no. 1401 or 1402)

Mark: Struck on spigot handle with maker's mark

Description: The curved U tube with parallel compression cylinder with plunger with loop handle; the spigot with shaped handle

H. 1 × W. 17 × D. 9¼ in. (2.5 × 43.2 × 23.5 cm)
Weight: 9 oz. 10 dwt. (299 g)

The silver wine siphon appears in the middle of the eighteenth century. This example follows the usual form of a curved tube with a spigot at the end; some, like this one, have a pump attached to force the wine through.[1] An example akin to this one was included in the exhibition *The Goldsmith and the Grape* in 1983.[2]

1   See Butler, *Wine*, p. 250.
2   Blair, p. 36.

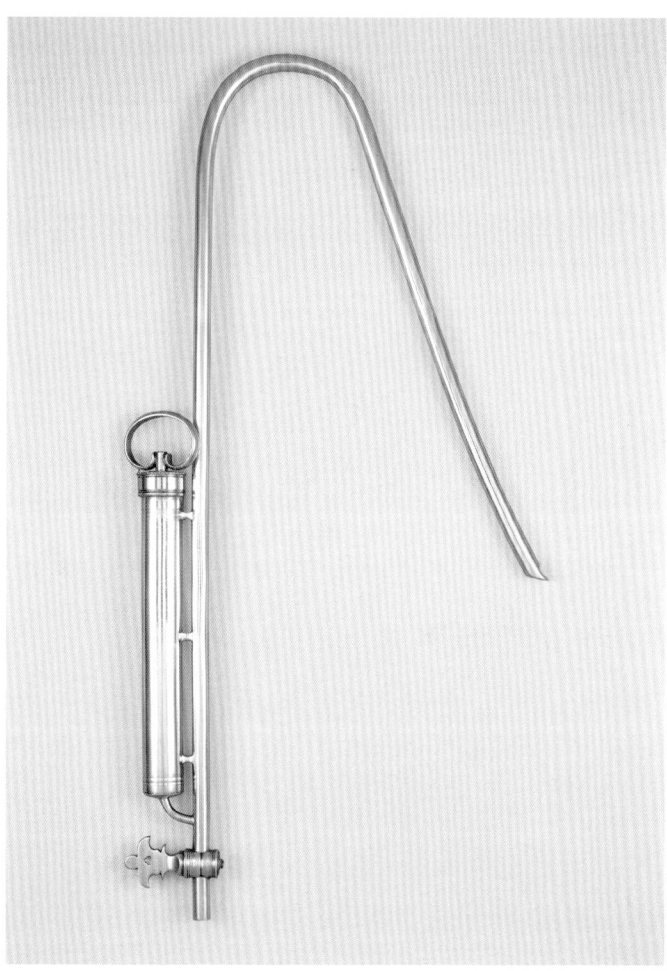

74

75, 76

75

Serving trowel

Silver (? sterling standard)

c. 1745

Maker's mark: Elizabeth Godfrey of London (Grimwade, no. 591)

Marks: Struck twice on the front of the blade with maker's mark

Description: With cannon handle, the blade approximating to the form of half a subellipse, pierced with stylized scrolls, rosettes and, in the centre, a square of crosses

H. 1½ × W. 13 × D. 4½ in. (4 × 33 × 11.5 cm)
Weight: 6 oz. 5 dwt. (195 g)

Heraldry: The crest is that of Ashley.

Serving trowels were used for a variety of foods and are uncommon before the middle of the eighteenth century. "One Silver Slice" is included in "A note of my Lady's plate in the buttery", part of an inventory of plate made at Knole in the 1660s.[1] The Earl of Kildare, owner of the nest of beakers (no. 78), purchased a "Pudding Trowle" in the same order from George Wickes in 1745. During the second half of the eighteenth century these serving implements proliferated and the fashion for eating whitebait in the 1770s inspired a host of trowels which, from their decoration, are obviously intended for fish rather than puddings. Five serving slices with elliptical blades from Paul de Lamerie's workshop are recorded, dating from the 1740s, all engraved with fish to denote their purpose.[2]

Elizabeth Godfrey was part of the tightly knit network of successful Huguenot makers in London. Her father was Simon Pantin (see no. 70), and her first husband was Abraham Buteux, whose business she continued after his death in 1731 until her marriage to Benjamin Godfrey, who appears to have been one of her late husband's journeymen. Benjamin then ran the business in Norris Street until his death in 1741, when Elizabeth entered her own mark, which appears on this object, at Goldsmiths' Hall. Her trade card proudly proclaims that she is "Goldsmith, Silversmith and Jeweller to His Royal Highness the Duke of Cumberland". Her workshop was prolific.

1 Sackville Papers, West Kent Record Office/U269/E69.
2 Rabinovitch, pp. 38–41.

76

Sauce ladle

Silver (? sterling standard)

Possibly Irish, c. 1780

Maker's mark: IC

Marks: Struck on back of stem with maker's mark, and STERLING

Description: The back of the circular bowl in the form of a shell; the tapering stem with shell terminal

H. 1⅝ × W. 7 × D. 2¼ in. (4 × 17.9 × 5.7 cm)
Weight: 8 oz. (250 g)

77

77

Pair of double spice boxes

Silver (sterling standard), interiors gilt

London, 1744/45

Maker's mark: George Methuen (Grimwade, no. 852)

Marks: Struck under bases with hallmarks (lion passant, leopard's head and date letter) and with maker's mark, the interiors of each cover with lion passant and maker's mark

Description: Shaped oblong with moulded borders, each raised on four scroll feet; each with central hinge and two flat covers; each one engraved with a coat of arms, crest and motto within a foliate scroll and rusticated cartouche flanked by floral garlands

H. 1⅞ × W. 5⅛ × D. 3¼ in. (4.8 × 13 × 8.3 cm)
Weight: 27 oz. 5 dwt. (850 g)

Heraldry: The arms are those of Hampden, as borne by John Hampden (1696–1754).

Provenance: John Hampden (1696–1754)

The functions given to these boxes with double flaps in contemporary inventories are often confusing, and may indicate the appraiser's own confusion. They are most frequently described as "pepper boxes" but the list made in 1760 of the late Earl of Leicester's plate mentions "One Double box for pepper and musterd",[1] while a "Silver gilt Salt Cellar with fflaps" is recorded in the use of the Gentleman of the Cellar between 1732 and 1749.[2]

John Hampden, the great-grandson of John Hampden, the Parliamentarian who opposed Charles I in the stormy years leading up to the Civil War, died unmarried at the age of 58 and left his estates at Great Hampden, Buckinghamshire, to his cousin, Robert Trevor, who as a result changed his name to Hampden and was created Viscount Hampden in 1776.

1 Murdoch, *Noble*, p. 238.
2 NA [PRO]/LC/9/45 f. 5.

78

Nest of six beakers

Silver (sterling standard), interiors gilt

London, 1745/46

Maker's mark: George Wickes (Grimwade, no. 927)

Marks: Struck under bases with hallmarks (lion passant, leopard's head and date letter) and with maker's mark

Description: With everted sides and rounded bases; the sides engraved with a crest and earl's coronet; the bases with scratch weights 7=3, 5=9, 5=3, 4=16, 3=14 and 3=16

H. 4 to 3¼ in. (10 to 8.3 cm) *Diam.* 3⅝ to 2⅞ in. (9 to 7.5 cm)
Weight: 28 oz. 15 dwt. (901 g)

77 coat of arms

78

Heraldry: The crest and coronet are those of James Fitzgerald, 20th Earl of Kildare (1722–1773).

Provenance: James Fitzgerald, 20th Earl of Kildare (1722–1773), created Duke of Leinster in 1766, by descent to Edward, 7th Duke of Leinster (1892–1976), (?) Sir Harry Mallaby-Deeley

James Fitzgerald was the premier peer of Ireland. He succeeded his father as Earl of Kildare, an Irish title, in 1743/44 and was given an English peerage, as Viscount Leinster of Taplow, by George II in 1746/47 following his marriage to Emilia, the daughter of the Duke of Richmond. This prompted Horace Walpole to quip that the bride's parents "have not given her a shilling, but the King endows her by making Lord Kildare a Viscount *sterling*". In 1766 he was created Duke of Leinster by George III.

Fitzgerald is of interest to silver scholars today because of his considerable purchases of plate from the eminent retailer, George Wickes. The dinner service he commissioned between 1745 and 1747 remains virtually intact and, comprising some 170 pieces, is the most extensive eighteenth-century dinner service in existence, weighing over 5,000 ounces. By a happy chance, the business ledgers of Wicke's firm survived being dumped in a builder's skip in the 1950s and are now in the Archive of Art and Design, part of the Victoria & Albert Museum.[1] Fitzgerald's dealings with Wickes are documented in Wickes's *Gentleman's Ledger*: his purchases during the two-year period amounted to some £3,669.

The year before he ordered his magnificent dinner service, Lord Kildare purchased a number of smaller articles of tea silver, including a set of twelve teacups and saucers, and personal items such as a nutmeg grater and this rare set of beakers:

The R^t. Honble. The Earl of Kildare Debtor
1745
September 17
To 6 Travelling Cups Guilt inside   30 – 2   6/2   9 = 5 = 8
To making and Guilding at £1 Each   6 = 0 = 0[2]

Sets of nesting beakers and tumblers had been popular since the Middle Ages and a number of sets made in England in the second half of the seventeenth century survive. But because of their utilitarian nature, they are rare survivals of what must have been a commonplace piece of personal silver. The Jewel Office delivery books record the following for August 21, 1728:

Deli^d. To the King's Hunstman by the Hands of Mr. Brudenell, Master of the Office, for His Majestys Service – viz. Four gilt Tumblers, one within another, & a Shagreen Case—
w^t. 19 – 13 – 0
Delivered by ye said James Brudenell to Rich^d. Aldworth Esqr. For ye use of y^e said Bottle carrier[3]

1 For a thorough account of Wickes's business, and the rescue of the business papers, see Barr; the Leinster dinner service is discussed in Appendix II.
2 AAD/1995/7/13 (VAM13).
3 NA [PRO]/LC/9/44 f. 261.

78 crest

The Domcha Collection

79

Egg frame

Silver (sterling standard)

Dublin, c. 1749/50

Maker's mark: JW without a pellet in rectangular punch (Bennett, no. 328), probably for John Wilme I

Mark: Struck on reverse with Hibernia, crowned harp (both Bennett, *Georgian*, p. 264, illustrated with date letter for 1749) and maker's mark

Description: Formed of six circular egg holders enclosing a central circular well, raised on three inwardly scrolling feet, the top engraved with a crest of lion jamb; engraved under the base with scratch weight 7=16-12

H. 1 1/8 × W. 5 1/2 × D. 5 in. (2.8 × 14 × 12.7 cm)
Weight: 7 oz. 10 dwt. (236 g)

Heraldry: The crest is common to a number of families but a likely candidate is the Newcomen family of Dublin.

The only other known surviving egg frame from the second quarter of the eighteenth century is a large London-made example of 1740/41 supplied by Peter Archambo to the 2nd Earl of Warrington.[1] It is raised up on scroll feet and fitted with ten egg cups. Like this Irish example, the Warrington example exploits the potential offered by geometry for visual effect: the ten circles are arranged 4, 3, 2, 1 as a triangle and, according to Lomax and Rothwell, the proportions are based on a ratio of 1:5.

This Irish example is arranged, like some English and Irish salvers of the period, as a hexafoil, providing a central circular well which no doubt was for salt. It was clearly never intended to have egg cups, as the eggs sit in the circular holders. Ceramic frames similar in form to this are known from the end of the seventeenth century, and in fact there are a few tantalizing references to silver egg frames in documents. In 1690 Lady Hervey recorded that "Dear Cosen donn gave me a silver ege thing worth ten ginnes", which must have been a good deal bigger than this example, which would have cost perhaps £4 or so.[2] The Jewel Office had an "egg stand" in 1702.[3] Egg frames or stands, usually fitted with egg cups, were produced in large numbers from the 1770s onwards, but this example is one of the two earliest known, and probably the only Irish example from before the 1780s.

Hens' eggs were considerably smaller in the eighteenth century, accounting for the comparatively small size of the circular holders. Eggs were eaten boiled, or coddled, by slicing the tops off with a knife: the Earl of Kildare's account with George Wickes for 1746/47 records the sale of "6 Egg Knives, Silver Blades" for £2 10s (see no. 78). Louis XV was said to be particularly adept at decapitating eggs.[4]

Dating this egg stand accurately is difficult because it lacks a date letter. The stamp of Hibernia was introduced in 1730 but, as Douglas Bennett observes, "With the innovation of the punch of Hibernia comes one of the most difficult periods for establishing a date anywhere in the British Isles, as for no apparent reason the assay office dropped the practice of applying a date letter to most articles of silver, with the exception of spoons and forks". Comparison of the crowned harp and Hibernia marks with existing pieces with date letters or documented dates is the only way to arrive at a date during the period 1730–1750. The Hibernia and crown harp marks struck on this egg frame are those used in 1749/50 in conjunction with the date letter for that year.

The identification of the Dublin maker's mark JW is also difficult as there are several goldsmiths working in Dublin during the middle years of the eighteenth century with these initials. Contenders for the mark *JW in upper-case roman letters without a pellet between* include John Williamson (fl. 1706–1736), John Wilme I (fl. 1718–1754), James Wilme II (? fl. 1753–1774), James Warren (fl. 1752–1789) and John West (fl. 1754–1806).[5] Given the date of this egg stand of around 1749/50, Williamson and Wilme are the only candidates out of this group.

Two marks that use the initials IW have traditionally been ascribed to Williamson: one incorporating a fleur-de-lis and another with scalloped top (Bennett, nos. 338 and 339), but the situation is by no means clear. Williamson was a Quarter Brother in 1706 and is recorded as a Freeman between 1716 and 1736. He was elected Junior Warden in 1729 but declined to serve. Williamson had only 95 ounces assayed in 1731/32 and none in the following nine months, and from then on he fades from the records. In contrast, John Wilme I had some 1,542 ounces assayed in 1747/48 (the records are missing for 1748–1752). A Huguenot, Wilme had been admitted a Quarter Brother of the Dublin guild in 1718.[6] He was finally made a Freeman in 1736, served as Warden of the Company 1736–1739 and was elected Master in 1739. He served on the Common Council of the city from 1749 onwards, and was Assay Master between 1751 and 1754. Thomas Sinsteden has observed: "John Wilme continued to be a productive goldsmith through 1748. In light of this, more silver assayed after 1732 with maker's mark IW should be attributed to John Wilme rather than John Williamson."[7]

1 Lomax and Rothwell, pp. 70–71, no. 21. It is now on display at the earl's house, Dunham Massey, in Cheshire.
2 Clayton, *Dictionary*, p. 167.
3 Lomax and Rothwell, p. 71.
4 Hernmark, p. 205.
5 See Bennett, pp. 171–2 and Bennett, *Georgian*, pp. 333–4.
6 T. Murdoch and T. Sinsteden, "Names of known, believed or possible Huguenot goldsmiths of Dublin", in T. Murdoch, ed., *Beyond the Border, Huguenot Goldsmiths in Northern Europe and North America*,

Eastbourne, 2008, p. 155. Quarter Brothers, as opposed to Freemen, were foreign workers, or those that did not belong to the established Protestant church. This last category included Huguenots as well as Roman Catholics.

7 Sinsteden, "Assay Records 2", p. 98.

80

Cream jug or cow creamer

Silver (sterling standard)

London, 1757/58

Maker's mark: John Schuppe (Grimwade, no. 1686)

Marks: Struck under body with hallmarks (lion passant, leopard's head, date letter) and with maker's mark

Description: Realistically modelled and chased as a cow, with hairy body and tail looped to form the handle; the hinged cover on her back chased with a band of flowers and surmounted by a bee

H. 4 × W. 6 × D. 1⅞ in. (10 × 15.2 × 4.8 cm)
Weight: 4 oz. 15 dwt. (152 g)

Small cow-shaped cream jugs for the tea table enjoyed a brief vogue in the 1750s and 60s. Almost without exception they are marked by John Schuppe, who appears to have been a Dutch immigrant, although no record of any apprenticeship or freedom of any livery company is known. He entered a mark as a largeworker in 1753 which appears almost exclusively on these cows, the only variety in them being that some have smooth bodies and others, like this example, are hairy.[1] The cows are modelled after ceramic creamers imported from the continent and copied by Stoke-on-Trent potters. Porcelain examples were made at the Longton Hall factory.

The cow creamer represents the broadening of the consumer base for silver during the middle years of the eighteenth century. In addition, the price of tea had dropped dramatically since 1700, enlarging the size of teapots and cream jugs. The tea table offered city merchants' wives and farmers' daughters the chance to display new wealth through porcelain cups and saucers and perhaps a silver cream jug and spoons. Whimsy played a large part in the decoration in this last phase of the English rococo. Cow creamers were probably sold in "toy shops", which were retail establishments selling luxury goods such as silver articles one might give as gifts, snuff-boxes and other personal items.

In the twentieth century, silver cow creamers were especially popular with collectors, In some of the comic novels of P. G. Wodehouse a cow creamer recurs as a symbol of the mad obsession of Uncle Tom, the silver collector who was married to Bertie Wooster's Aunt Dahlia – "This cow-creamer, in case you're interested, was a silver jug or pitcher or whatever you call it shaped, of all silly things, like a cow with an arching tail and a juvenile-delinquent expression on its face, a cow that looked as if it were planning, next time it was milked, to haul off and let the milkmaid have it in the lower ribs. Its back opened on a hinge and the tip of the tail touched the spine, thus giving the householder something to catch hold of when pouring. Why anyone would want such a revolting object had always been a mystery to me, it ranking high up on the list of things I would have been reluctant to be found dead in a ditch with, but apparently they liked that sort of thing in the eighteenth century and, coming down to more modern times, Uncle Tom was all for it …"[2]

1 For an example of one with a smooth body, see Wark, p. 68, no. 165.
2 P. G. Wodehouse, *Jeeves in the Offing*, London, 1960, p. 59.

The Domcha Collection

81

Sweetmeat basket

Silver (sterling standard)

London, 1761/62

Maker's mark: John Parker I & Edward Wakelin (Grimwade, no. 1602)

Marks: Struck under base with hallmarks (lion passant, leopard's head, date letter) and with maker's mark, the underside of the handle with lion passant

Description: Elliptical on spreading foot cast and chased as openwork trailing flowers; the everted sides pierced with spiral panels of alternating ovolos and trellis, the flat rim applied with trailing flowers, the overhead swing handle cast as a trailing vine

H. 5½ × W. 7⅜ × D. 6¼ in. (14 × 18.7 × 16 cm)
Weight: 9 oz. 15 dwt. (303 g)

Such delightful small baskets were probably used for sugar as part of the tea equipage. A similar basket forms part of a service of tea silver supplied by Paul de Lamerie for the Franks family of Philadelphia.[1] Others are found in sets of four hanging from the scrolling branches of epergnes.

John Parker and Edward Wakelin took over the retailing business started by George Wickes (see no. 78) in Panton Street, Westminster, and their partnership continued until 1776.

1 Hartop, *Huguenot*, pp. 312–17.

82

Four fluted dishes and covers

Silver (sterling standard)

London: the dishes 1758/59; the covers 1769/70

Maker's mark: Frederick Kandler (Grimwade, no. 692)

Marks: Struck on sides and on cover flanges with hallmarks (lion passant, leopard's head, date letter) and with maker's mark

80, 81

Description: Oblong octangular, the deep sides, with scalloped rim, chased with radiating flutes, eight of which straddle the corners; each dish with two loop handles; the fluted slightly domed covers with fluted melon finial; the centres engraved with a coat of arms within a scroll and *rocaille* cartouche flanked by Chinese urns and flowers, the covers engraved with a crest

H. 3⅞ × W. 10¾ × D. 7¼ in. (9.8 × 27.3 × 18.4 cm)
Weight: 123 oz. (3848 g)

Heraldry: The arms are those of Meynell quartering those of Poyntz and Littleton and impaling those of Boothby quartering those of Skrymshire, for Hugo Meynell (1727 or 1735–1808) of Bradley, Derbyshire and Quorn Hall, Leicestershire.

Provenance: Hugo Meynell (1727 or 1735–1808), by descent to Major Hugo Meynell of Hoar Cross, Burton-on-Trent, sale, Christie's, London, July 24, 1946; Thomas Lumley, 1957; A New York Collector, sale, Sotheby's, October 24, 2000, lot 326

Published: Clayton, *Dictionary*, p. 171, fig. 258

These highly unusual dishes and covers rely on their fluting for effect. Radiating flutes and shaped rims are often found on circular or elliptical "sallet" dishes during the first half of the eighteenth century, but these dishes appear to be the only ones of this oblong octangular form recorded. Similar fluting adorns a pair of *verrières* or montieths made for the same patron, supplied by Frederick Kandler in 1776/77, now in the Carnegie Museum of Art, Pittsburgh.

The Meynells were a Derbyshire family whose landholdings had been greatly increased by Francis Meynell, a successful goldsmith banker in London who bought the Bradley estate in 1655. His grandson, Littleton Poyntz Meynell (c. 1695–1752), married Judith Alleyne, a rich heiress from Barbados, in 1720. Littleton has been described as an arrogant man and an unscrupulous but highly successful gambler. Horace Walpole observed that he "had created a large fortune at play, and nobody doubted but by unfair play".[1] In about 1730, Littleton began buying plate from Henry Jernegan, a goldsmith banker at the Sign of the Sun in Great Russell Street. Much of this silver has survived and, almost without exception, it is struck with the mark of Charles Kandler, a German immigrant silversmith who had arrived in London in 1727 and had premises at the Sign of the Mitre in Jermyn Street.[2] Meynell's greatest commission from Jernegan – and perhaps the largest English silver object to survive from the eighteenth century – was the great wine cistern designed by George Vertue, modelled by John Michael Rysbrack and made by Charles Kandler, weighing some 7,700 ounces, now in St Petersburg. However, on its completion Meynell refused to take delivery of the cistern and it became the subject of bitter litigation between Meynell and Jernegan.[3]

Despite this rift between the retailer and his client, Littleton Meynell's son, Hugo, appears to have continued his family's patronage of the Kandler shop for several decades after his father's death. Hugo was the second son but had inherited his father's estates in 1752 after his elder brother had been cut out of his father's will. Hugo Meynell served as High Sheriff of Derbyshire in 1758 and sat as an MP between 1761 and 1778, but it is as a foxhunter that he is best known. Establishing himself at Quorn Hall in Leicestershire in 1753, he hunted the surrounding country with a legendary pack of hounds which, it was said, he bred on new scientific principles

The Domcha Collection

82 coat of arms

of selective breeding. Foxhunting as a fashionable sport with fixed "countries" assigned to each pack of hounds owes its development to Meynell, who hunted until his death in 1808.[4] Meynell's second marriage in 1758 to Ann Boothby Skrymshire, daughter and heiress of another local landowner, greatly increased his local influence and his wealth. These dishes evidently formed part of their marriage plate.

Keeping virtually open house at Quorn during the hunting season, Meynell found that his fame as a Master of Hounds and as a host meant that he and his pack were besieged by eager sportsmen. In response to this, sets of rooms were made available to guests who paid for their own food and drink which were, reputedly, served in great profusion. In contrast, however, in an age of excess, Meynell's own habits were abstemious: "His usual hunting breakfast consisted of as much as a small tea-cup would contain of a pound of veal, condensed to that quantity. His pocket was always fortified with a bottle of stimulus, similar to that commonly carried at

Hugo Meynell (1727 or 1735–1808) by Sir Joshua Reynolds, oil on canvas. *Christie's Images*

the present day; but instead of eau-de-vie, curaçao, or cherry-bounce, it contained a far better stomachic, in the shape of veritable tincture of rhubarb, to the use of which he was constantly addicted".[5]

The genealogy of the Kandler family in London is uncertain. Charles Kandler, the founder of the shop, appears to have returned to Dresden by 1735 when he is recorded in the visitor's book at the Meissen porcelain factory, where his putative brother, Johann Joachim Kändler, was chief modeller. Meissen porcelain from 1735 onwards, with its *bombé* bodies and vertical fluting, is very similar to the silver Kandler had produced in London, lending weight to Maureen Cassidy-Geiger's suggestion that Charles subsequently "provided advice and design expertise to his brother in the production of the Sulkowski service".[6] The shop in Jermyn Street was continued by Charles Frederick Kandler, probably a nephew of Charles, who, sometime in the 1740s, appears to have dropped the first Christian name. Frederick Kandler supplied well-made plate to many of the aristocracy and gentry in the 1750s, 60s and 70s. A bill made out to Lady Stanhope dated April 28, 1760, has a printed heading: "Frederick Kandler, Goldsmith, against St. James's-Church, Jermain Street".[7] He died in 1778 and the business was continued by his son Charles.[8]

One of a pair of *verrières*, silver, London, 1776/77, mark of Frederick Kandler, engraved with the same arms. *Carnegie Museum of Art, Pittsburgh*

1. Cameron, p. 488.
2. Littleton Meynell's silver from Kandler, all of it in the sculptural style for which his workshop is well known, includes a pair of soup tureens with horse-head handles, c.1730, in the Cahn Collection (Alcorn, *Lamerie*, p. 49, no. 3), a pair of candlesticks, 1730/31, in the Hartman Collection, Museum of Fine Arts, Boston (Hartop, *Huguenot*, p. 380, no. 100), a kettle on lampstand, c.1730, in the Victoria & Albert Museum, London (Alcorn, *Lamerie*, p. 52, fig. 3-7), and other items included in Property of Major Hugo Meynell of Hoar Cross, Burton-on-Trent, sale, Christie's, London, July 24, 1946, cited in Cameron, p. 500.
3. The litigation and the subsequent fate of the wine cooler are discussed in detail in Cameron, pp. 487–93.
4. Meynell's posthumous fame was largely due to the nineteenth-century journalist Charles James Apperley (Nimrod). For an account of Meynell's contribution to hunting, see Raymond Carr, *English Foxhunting: a History*, London, 1976; much of the Meynell "legend" is debunked in I. Middleton, "Fox Hunting Traditions: Fact or Fantasy?" *Sport History Review*, no. 28, 1997, pp. 19–32.
5. Colin D.B. Ellis, *Leicestershire and the Quorn Hunt*, Leicester, 1951, p. 19.
6. Cassidy-Geiger, "Sugar and silver", p. 154.
7. West Kent Record Office, Stanhope Papers/U1590/E14.
8. Cameron, p. 498.

83
Dish

Silver (950/1000 standard)

Auch (Juridiction de Bayonne)

c.1760

Maker's mark: Jean Affre I (Helft, no. 206d)

Marks: Struck on reverse with hallmark (town mark) and with maker's mark

Description: Circular with ruled rim and raised sides, with two double-scroll handles riveted to the rim

H. 2½ × W. 12¼ × D. 10¾ in. (6.4 × 31.2 × 27.3 cm)
Weight: 26 oz. (813 g)

Jean Affre was the son of Étienne Affre who had been admitted a master in Toulouse, the nearest major gold-smithing centre, in 1723. Jean was received as a freeman of Auch in 1754 and was still working there in 1799. Jacques Helft dates this version of his maker's mark to the 1760s.

Rare in English silver, plain circular dishes with two

The Domcha Collection

handles were popular in eighteenth-century France. Interestingly, the handles on this dish are riveted, a technique which did not require a large-scale furnace or accurate regulation of the soldering temperature.

84

Pair of condiment pots

Silver (? sterling standard)

Mid-eighteenth century

Maker's mark: WC in rectangular punch with canted corners, probably for William Cripps of London (cf. Grimwade, no. 3058)

Marks: Struck under bases with maker's mark

Description: Plain cylindrical with flat hinged covers and heavy scroll handles; the covers engraved with a viscount's coronet over a crest of ostrich plumes out of a ducal coronet, one inscribed below PEPPER, the other MUSTARD; all within ruled borders, with clear-glass liners, and two plain spoons, London, 1993/94, maker's mark of S.J. Phillips

H. 3 × W. 3¾ × D. 2⅝ in. (7.6 × 9.5 × 6.5 cm)
Weight of pots: 10 oz. 12 dwt. (330 g)

Heraldry: The crest and coronet are those of Richard, 4th Viscount Howe, the celebrated Admiral of the Fleet. Born in 1726, he succeeded his brother as Viscount Howe in 1758 and was created Earl Howe in 1788.

Provenance: Richard, 4th Viscount Howe (1726–1799), by descent to his youngest daughter Louisa Catherine, who married John, 1st Marquess of Sligo (1756–1809), by descent to Denis, 10th Marquess of Sligo (1908–1991), sale, Christie's, London, May 13, 1953, lot 158; Nathaniel, 3rd Baron Rothschild (1910–1990)

For a discussion of the use of ground mustard and mustard paste, see no. 33. From the middle of the century, mustard pots, or "mustard tankards", appear in Parker and Wakelin's ledgers and various goldsmiths' bills, no doubt referring to vessels such as these. In 1777 the London Assay Office charged 1½d for hallmarking "mustard cans".[1] Among the earliest "mustard cans" of this form with hallmarks is one of 1758/59 with the mark of Edward Wakelin, formerly in the Colman Collection.[2] A mustard pot of similar form to this pair, with the same maker's mark and also without hallmarks, was formerly in the Albert Collection.[3]

1 Godfrey, p. 16.
2 Ibid, p. 21, no. 2.
3 Butler, *Albert*, p. 83, no. 97.

85

Inkstand

Silver (sterling standard)

Dublin, 1770/71

Maker's mark: John Craig (Bennett, p. 167, column 1, line 5)

Marks: Struck inside central well with hallmarks (harp, Hibernia, date letter) and with maker's mark; the taperstick with harp and Hibernia

Description: Rectangular with moulded border, on four bracket feet, with flat tab handle with baluster terminal and two cylindrical pots, one for ink with hinged cap, the other for sand with pierced cover, flanking a taperstick with cylindrical socket and tab handle

84

H. 2⅛ × W. 5½ × D. 5 in. (5.4 × 14 × 12.7 cm)
Weight: 8 oz. 12 dwt. (270 g)

Small inkstands of this type appear in England in the late 1720s. One of 1732/33, mark of Edward Feline, and another of 1744/45, mark of John Eckford, were sold from the collection of Elizabeth Parke Firestone, Christie's, New York, March 23, 1991, lots 837 and 836 respectively.

86

Saucepan

Silver (sterling standard), fruitwood

Dublin, 1715/20

Maker's mark: Edward Workman (Bennett, p. 164, column 2, line 4)

Marks: Struck under base with hallmarks (harp, date letter) and with maker's mark

Description: Cylindrical with moulded rim, straight turned baluster wooden handle; engraved under the base with scratch weight *8=18*

H. 5½ × W. 7¾ × D. 4½ in. (14 × 19.6 × 11.5 cm)
Gross weight: 9 oz. 5 dwt. (289 g)

This saucepan bears the Dublin date letter of a lower-case Gothic a, which has always been ascribed to 1717/18. However, there are not enough letters in alphabetical sequence to fill the years between 1715 and 1722 changing the letter each year, and the large number of pieces which survive struck with the "a" suggests that it was used for more than one year. In 1999 research by Ida Delamer and Conor O'Brien, based on examination of church silver for which there is documentation regarding its commissioning or donation, was published which concluded that this letter should be given the years 1717 to 1720.[1]

The discrepancy between this object's current weight and that engraved on its base is explained by the fact that scratch weights usually denote the weight of silver, without any wooden handle.

1 Delamer and O'Brien, pp. 158–67.

87

Argyll

Silver (sterling standard), fruitwood

London, 1773/74

Maker's mark: John Carter (Grimwade, cf. no. 1214)

Marks: Struck under the base with hallmarks (lion passant, leopard's head, date letter) and with maker's mark, the side with lion passant, the cover flange with lion passant and maker's mark

Description: Cylindrical with tubular scroll spout and wooden loop handle at right angles; the hinged slightly domed cover with acorn finial and hot-water cap by the hinge

H. 5⅛ × W. 5¾ × D. 6¼ in. (13 × 14.6 × 16 cm)
Gross weight: 15 oz. (467 g)

The Domcha Collection

87, 86

88

Geometry and the Silversmith

The 3rd Duke of Argyll (1682–1761), no doubt shivering in his castle dining-room at Inveraray, is credited with the invention, in the middle years of the eighteenth century, of a gravy pot with an inner sleeve to contain hot water. Josiah Wedgwood marketed ceramic examples which he called "gravy cups". Among the earliest silver examples is one of 1755/56 with the mark of Fuller White.[1]

1 Harold Newman, "Argylls – Silver and Ceramic", *Apollo*, February, 1969, p. 98.

This saucepan and cover copy contemporary copper examples found in the kitchen, and were clearly intended to be used by the cook. Two similar examples, also from a ducal household, bear the arms of the 10th Duke of Hamilton, and are struck with Glasgow hallmarks for 1845/46 and the mark of Robert Gray & Son.[1]

1 One is in the Kelvingrove Museum, Glasgow, and illustrated in Dalgleish and Steuart Fothringham, p. 110, no. 5.54; the other was sold Sotheby's, Gleneagles, August 28, 1988, lot 474.

88
Saucepan and cover

Silver (sterling standard)

London, 1773/74

Maker's mark: Sebastian Crespell I & James Crespell (Grimwade, no. 2497)

Marks: Struck under base and on interior of cover with hallmarks (lion passant, leopard's head, date letter) and with maker's mark

Description: Cylindrical with straight pointed handle; the dished cover with smaller similar handle; the front and cover engraved with a crest within the Order of the Garter and surmounted by a duke's coronet; both handle flanges with scratch weight *38"3*

H. 7 × W. 15½ × D. 6⅞ in. (17.8 × 39.4 × 17.5 cm)
Weight: 36 oz. 15 dwt. (1143 g)

Heraldry: The crest and coronet are those of George Montagu, formerly Brudenell, 1st Duke of Montagu (1712–1790).

Provenance: George, 1st Duke of Montagu (1712–1790); The James Walker Collection of Silver and Vertu, sale, Christie's, South Kensington, July 13, 2006, lot 187

89
Saucepan

Silver (sterling standard), fruitwood

York, 1784/85

Maker's mark: John Hampston & John Prince (Jackson, p. 464, line 1)

Marks: Struck under base with hallmarks (town mark, lion passant, leopard's head, date letter, duty mark) and with maker's mark

Description: Circular with rounded base and straight turned wooden handle issuing from a heart-shaped calyx

H. 6 × W. 16½ × D. 7 in. (15.2 × 42 × 17.8 cm)
Gross weight: 19 oz. 15 dwt. (613 g)

John Hampston and John Prince had been journeyman and apprentice respectively of the York goldsmith Ambrose Beckwith from whose widow they purchased the business in Coney Street in 1770.[1] Hampston and Prince went on to be the largest shop in the city and following the re-opening of the York Assay Office in 1776 they supplied local demand

89

The Domcha Collection

with a wide range of small domestic articles made in their workshops. Most of their own wares were items of flatware and wine labels, and this saucepan is among the larger articles they made. The "Tea Kitchens, Tureens, Cups with Covers, Bread Baskets, [and] Candlesticks" they advertised were probably made in London, Birmingham or Sheffield and retailed in their shop.[2]

1   Murray, p. 66.
2   Gubbins, p. 12.

90
Saucepan and cover

Silver (sterling standard), fruitwood

London, 1786/87

Maker's mark: John Wakelin & William Tayler (Grimwade, no. 1764)

Marks: Struck under base with hallmarks (lion passant, leopard's head, date letter, duty mark) and with maker's mark, the interior of the cover with lion passant, duty mark and maker's mark

Description: With bowed sides and moulded rim, short spout and straight turned wooden handle at right angles issuing from a heart-shaped calyx; the slightly domed cover with turned wooden finial; the front engraved with a crest, the base with scratch weight *30=8*

H. 8 × W. 14 × D. 7 in. (20.3 × 35.5 × 17.8 cm)
Gross weight: 32 oz. 5 dwt. (1007 g)

Heraldry: The crest, that of a cock, pertains to a number of families, including Hallifax and Thoyt.

John Wakelin and William Tayler entered into a partnership in 1777 to run the successful retailing establishment started by George Wickes in the 1730s. John Wakelin was the son of Edward Wakelin, who had joined Wickes in 1747. They continued the practice of outsourcing silverware from a host of specialist suppliers.

90

91

Casserole and cover

Silver (sterling standard), fruitwood

London, 1787/88

Maker's mark: John Wakelin & William Tayler (Grimwade, no. 1764)

Marks: Struck under base with hallmarks (lion passant, leopard's head, date letter, duty mark) and with maker's mark, the cover flange with lion passant, duty mark and maker's mark

Description: Circular with moulded rim, straight turned wooden handle issuing from a heart-shaped calyx, the interior fitted into three compartments; the partially domed cover with vase-shaped finial headed by stiff foliage; the side and cover engraved with a crest within the Order of the Garter and surmounted by a viscount's coronet, the base with scratch weight *63=19*

H. 5½ × W. 10½ × D. 10 in. (14 × 26.7 × 25.4 cm)
Gross weight: 63 oz. 5 dwt. (1967 g)

Heraldry: The crest and coronet are those of Thomas, 3rd Viscount Weymouth, later 1st Marquess of Bath (1734–1796).

Provenance: Thomas, 3rd Viscount Weymouth and 1st Marquess of Bath, by descent to Alexander, 7th Marquess of Bath (b. 1932), the Trustees of the Longleat Chattels Settlement, sale, Christie's, London, June 13, 2002, lot 407

For a note about the business of Wakelin and Tayler, see no. 90. Their *Gentleman's Ledger* records:

Lord Vis' Weymouth 1787
Aug 24

To a large Casserole with 3 divisions and cover	
63 oz 19 dwt 8/6 gr	£27 3
To handle 1/6 duty 32 Eng 2 crests Garter & Cors @ 1/6	£2 3s[1]

The Duke of Montrose received four casseroles and covers weighing a total of nearly 232 ounces from the Jewel Office in 1794, in addition to his meat dishes and candlesticks. These were probably of the same form as this example.

A pair of similar casseroles and covers of 1809/10, mark of Robert and Samuel Hennell, is in the collection of Her Majesty The Queen.[2]

1 AAD/1995/7/18 (VAM 18).
2 Grimwade, *Queen's*, p. 102, no. 46.

The Domcha Collection

92

Four meat dishes

Silver (sterling standard)

London, 1794/95

Maker's mark: Henry Chawner (Grimwade, no. 971)

Marks: Struck on reverses with hallmarks (lion passant, leopard's head, date letter) and with maker's mark

Description: In four sizes, elliptical with plain flat borders; engraved with a coat of arms surmounted by a earl's coronet and opposite with the royal badge of George III enclosed by the Order of the Garter and surmounted by a crown; the reverses numbered and with scratch weights: *No. 1 = 80..5, No. 3 = 56..12, No. 5 = 37* and *No. 8 = 26..4*

H. 1½ to ¾ in. (3.8 to 2 cm) W. 22 to 15¼ in. (56 to 38.7 cm)
D. 16 to 10½ in. (40.6 to 26.7 cm)
Weight: 187 oz. (5842 g)

Heraldry: The arms are those of John, 4th Earl of Bute (1744–1814).

Provenance: John, 4th Earl and 1st Marquess of Bute (1744–1814)

John Stuart inherited the earldom of Bute on the death of his father, the Prime Minister and mentor of the young George III, in 1792. As Viscount Mount-Stuart he was envoy to Turin from 1779 until 1783 when he was sent as ambassador to Spain. He returned to London later that year but was sent again to Madrid in 1795. These dishes probably form part of the ambassadorial dinner service issued to him at that time. This severely plain form enjoyed a brief vogue at the end of the eighteenth century, and cost may well have been a factor in the use of this style for ambassadorial services. The Jewel Office had been closed in 1782 and its functions absorbed into the Lord Chamberlain's Office following an investigation over costs.[1] There were many more ambassadors and envoys to equip than there had been fifty years earlier, and the American Revolution had been a tremendous financial drain on the government. William Jones, of the retailing firm of Jeffries and Jones, had been appointed Principal Goldsmith to the Crown in 1783 and, as seen by these dishes, he farmed out the commissions to large-scale manufacturers such as Henry Chawner.[2] The plainness of these dishes contrasts sharply with the extravagant rococo creations from Thomas Heming's workshop that Lord Bute's father had received from the Jewel Office in the 1760s.

In 1796 Lord Bute was created Marquess of Bute. His first marriage, to Jane, daughter of Lord Windsor, had brought the family valuable estates around Cardiff in south Wales. After her death in 1800 he married Frances, the daughter of Thomas Coutts, the eminent banker. Their son's marriage to the only child of the Earl of Dumfries brought the family further extensive estates in Scotland, and Dumfries House.

92

The Domcha Collection

1 Lomax, p. 139.
2 See Sitwell, p. 152; for Jeffries and Jones, see Hartop, *Rundell*, p. 30. The service was extended in 1800: four large circular dishes matching these elliptical dishes, hallmarked 1800/01 and with the mark of John Emes, were sold, Property of a Gentleman, Christie's, London, May 4, 1977, lot 173, and twelve dinner plates with the same marks, also from the same service, were sold, Property of a Midwestern Collector, Christie's, New York, April 18, 1991, lot 324. A suite of six circular salvers, also of 1800/01 with the mark of Crouch and Hannam, was sold in Works of Art from the Bute Collection, Christie's, London, July 3, 1996, lot 95. These have the same engraved coat of arms and coronet, and dentelated borders.

93
Pail

Silver (sterling standard)

London, 1794/95

Maker's mark: John Wakelin & Robert Garrard I (Grimwade, no. 1760)

Marks: Struck under base with hallmarks (lion passant, leopard's head, date letter) and with maker's mark, the handle with lion passant and maker's mark

Description: Modelled on a milking pail, inverted truncated conical, applied with horizontal hoops, with overhead swing handle; the front engraved with a coat of arms and crest

H. 8 × Diam. 5 in. (20.4 × 12.8 cm)
Weight: 16 oz. (500 g)

Heraldry: The arms are those of Hase of Norfolk, with those of Repps on an escutcheon of pretence, as borne by Edward Hase (d. 1804).

Provenance: Edward Hase of Salle Park, Norfolk (1732–1804)

The function of this pail is unclear. It is just large enough to contain a narrow wine bottle, but it is perhaps more likely that it was intended for ice, or ice cream. Unfortunately the client ledger of the firm which would have recorded purchases by the Hase family does not appear to have survived among the Wickes/Parker/Wakelin/Tayler/Garrard records in the Archive of Art and Design (see p. 91).

Edward Hase of Salle, Norfolk, was the second son of John Hase of East Dereham and his wife Mary Lombe. Hase married Vertue Repps, an heiress, in 1754. Their daughter Vertue in 1772 married Richard Paul Jodrell MP, and had a son, also Richard Paul, who in 1817 succeeded to the baronetcy of Lombe (created in 1784) from his paternal great uncle, John Hase, who had changed his name to Lombe in 1762 in accordance with the will of his grandmother. Edward Hase built Salle Park in 1761, a large redbrick classical house with an armorial pediment.

94
Two ladles

Silver (sterling standard), fruitwood

London, 1798/99

Maker's mark: Paul Storr (Grimwade, no. 2235)

Marks: Struck on rims with hallmarks (lion passant, leopard's head, date letter, duty mark) and with maker's mark

Description: Elliptical in elevation, circular in plan, with short spouts, with turned wooden handles at right angles

H. 4 and 3¾ in. (10 and 9.5 cm)
W. 18¼ and 16 in. (46.4 and 40.6 cm)
D. 8¾ and 7⅝ in. (22.2 and 20 cm)
Gross weights: 32 oz. 15 dwt. and 26 oz. 18 dwt. (1018 and 837 g)

93

94

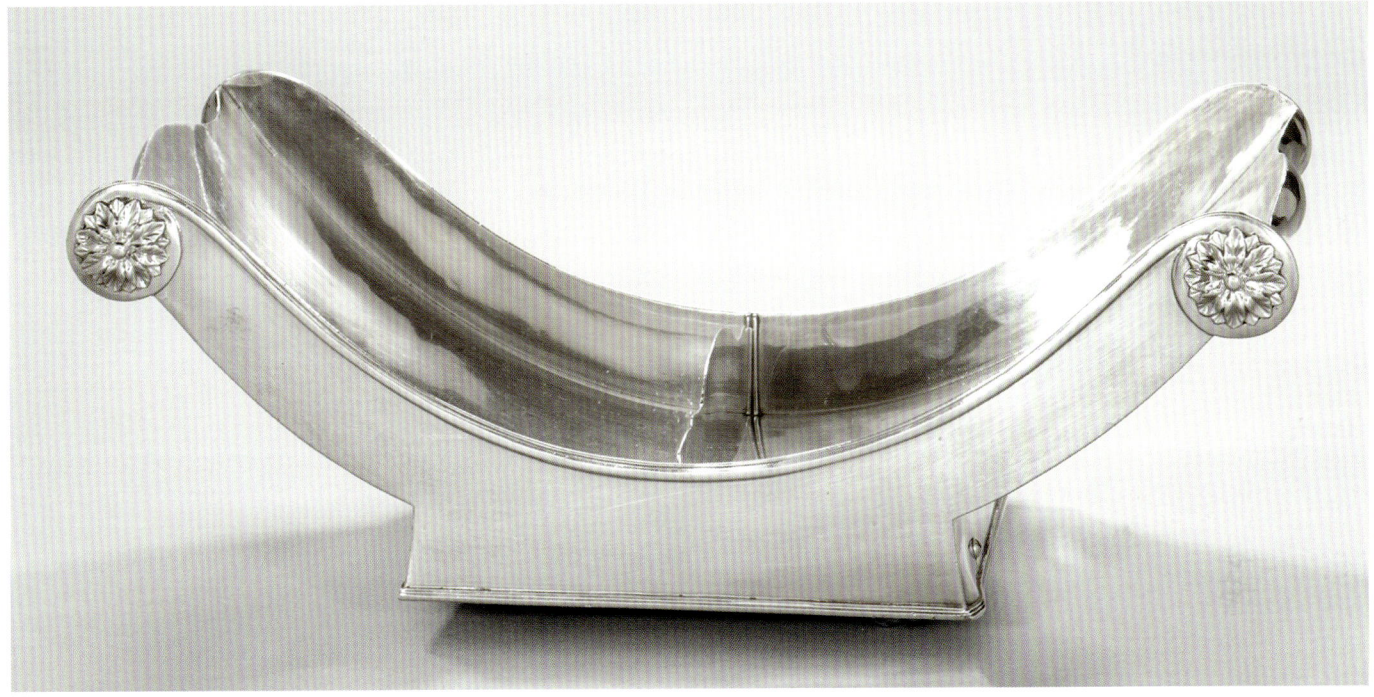

95

Provenance: Presumably Archibald, 9th Duke of Hamilton (1740–1819), then by descent to His Grace the Duke of Hamilton and Brandon, sale, Sotheby's, June 24, 1983, lots 298 and 299

Published: Clayton, *Dictionary*, p. 329

These starkly functional ladles were probably for use in the ducal kitchen (see no. 88), although in the absence of any engraved arms or crest, there is a possibility that their original owner was not the Duke of Hamilton but William Beckford (1760–1843), the aesthete and collector who was also a customer of Storr from 1800 onwards. Beckford's daughter Euphemia married Archibald, 10th Duke of Hamilton, and through her much of Beckford's silver and other collections came to the Hamilton family.

Paul Storr had been apprenticed to Andrew Fogelberg and entered his first mark, in partnership with William Frisbee, in 1792. He entered a new mark, alone, the following year.

By 1798 he was established in Air Street, Soho, making large-scale works with a superb finish. It is Storr's business arrangement with the royal goldsmiths, Rundell, Bridge and Rundell, from 1808 onwards that established his fame as the chief exponent of the Imperial style fashionable in the first quarter of the nineteenth century.

95

Cheese stand

Silver (sterling standard), fruitwood, brass

London, 1798/99

Maker's mark: Solomon Hougham (Grimwade, no. 2536)

Marks: Struck on one end with hallmarks (lion passant, leopard's head, date letter) and with maker's mark

The Domcha Collection

Description: Oblong boat-shaped with reeded borders, raised on four brass castors, each end applied with paterae, with removable central divider, wooden base

H. 6 × W. 16 × D. 7½ in. (15.2 × 40.6 × 19 cm)
Gross weight: 68 oz. 10 dwt. (2136 g)

Georgian cradles to hold a portion of a wheel of cheese are extremely rare in silver, though relatively common in mahogany. Four examples from the middle of the eighteenth century, all supplied either by Edward Wakelin or by his successors, Parker and Wakelin, are known. They all have elaborately pierced sides. One of these, supplied to the Earl of Coventry in 1755, appears in Wakelin's ledgers as "a Pierc'd Cheese Frame". Only a few plain boat-shaped examples from the end of the century, such as this, are known.[1]

1 They are: an example of 1754/55, Edward Wakelin, supplied to the Earl of Coventry, sold, Property of a Mid-Western Collector, Christie's, New York, October 30, 1990, lot 343; two of 1764/65, Edward Wakelin, supplied to the Earl of Exeter, one was sold by Christie's, London, July 6, 1966, the other in the Victoria & Albert Museum; and another of the same date, Parker and Wakelin, the Untermyer Collection, The Metropolitan Museum of Art, illustrated in Hackenbroch, p. 96, no. 186.

96

Pair of serving spoons and a fork

Silver (sterling standard)

London, 1799/1800

Maker's mark: Peter & Ann Bateman (Grimwade, no. 2140)

Marks: Struck on the back of the stems with hallmarks (lion passant, leopard's head, date letter, duty mark) and with maker's mark

96

Description: With long plain tapering stems, the fork with four prongs; the front of the stems engraved *Coll: Exon: Oxon. 1799*

The spoons:
H. 1¾ × W. 14⅛ × D. 2⅛ in. (4.4 × 35.9 × 5.4 cm)

The fork:
H. 1½ × W. 12¾ × D. 1¾ in. (3.8 × 32.4 × 4.4 cm)
Weight: 15 oz. 15 dwt. (489 g)

Provenance: Exeter College, Oxford

The Bateman firm supplied various silver items to Exeter College during the 1790s including a soup tureen and cover in 1790, paid for by a bequest of Benjamin Langley, which are still part of the college's collection.[1]

1 *Oxford Plate*, p. 64, no. 356.

97

Nutmeg grater with corkscrew

Silver (sterling silver), steel

London, 1803/04

Maker's mark: William Parker (Grimwade, no. 3265)

Marks: Struck on interior of vase with hallmarks (lion passant, leopard's head, date letter, duty mark) and with maker's mark, the interior of cap with lion passant

Description: Elliptical vase-shaped with hinged cap with ball finial, hinged to open revealing a steel grater, the lower part a cylindrical sheath unscrewing to reveal a corkscrew with steel helical worm

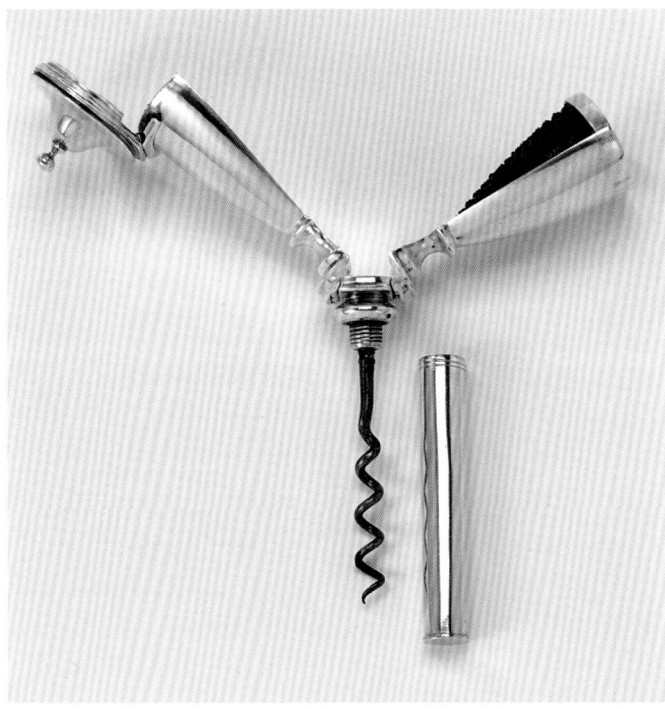

97

H. 5¼ × W. 1⅝ × D. 1¼ in. (13.3 × 4.1 × 3.1 cm)
Gross weight: 2 oz. 6 dwt. (71 g)

Provenance: The Albert Collection

Published: Butler, *Albert*, p. 60, no. 736

Nutmeg, a vital ingredient of punch, was grated at the table often using a portable grater. The idea of combining a corkscrew and nutmeg grater appears to date from the end of the eighteenth century and such compendia are particularly English.[1]

A similar vase-shaped nutmeg grater with corkscrew, of 1817/18, mark of Thomas and John Phipps, is in the Miles Collection.[2] It is evident that the Phipps family put together travelling canteens that included nutmeg graters, sold in fitted leather cases, and it is likely that they retailed graters made in the workshop of William Parker. A similar grater with corkscrew at Colonial Williamsburg, also with the mark of Parker, forms part of a travelling set with other components with the mark of Eley and Fearn, of 1803/04.[3]

1 Watney and Babbidge, p. 39.
2 Miles, p. 73, no. 46.
3 Davis, *Nutmegs*, p. 30, no. 35.

98

Honey skep, cover and stand

Silver gilt (sterling standard)

London 1809/10

Maker's mark: Rebecca Emes & Edward Barnard I (Grimwade, no. 2309)

Marks: Struck under base and on reverse of stand with hallmarks (lion passant, leopard's head, date letter, duty mark) and with maker's mark; the cover flanges struck with lion passant and maker's mark

Description: Realistically formed as a skep, with tied reeded borders, the removable cover surmounted by a bee, on circular matching stand

H. 5 × Diam. 5½ in. (12.7 × 14 cm)
Weight: 21 oz. 15 dwt. (682 g)

Heraldry: The crests and coronet are those of Richard, 1st Earl Howe (1796–1870).

Provenance: Richard, 1st Earl Howe (1796–1870)

Richard Curzon was the only son of Penn Curzon and his wife, Sophia Charlotte, Baroness Howe, who had inherited the title from her father, the famous Admiral. In 1821 Curzon was created Earl Howe. The consummate courtier, he was appointed Lord of the Bedchamber to Adelaide, Duchess of Clarence, in 1829, the year before her husband succeeded his brother, George IV, as King William IV. Howe continued to

The Domcha Collection

98

serve Queen Adelaide long after the death of the king in 1837, and their mutual devotion gave rise to scurrilous rumours that they were lovers. Lord Howe had a magnificent collection of silver-gilt plate which was dispersed by his descendants in auction sales in 1933 and 1953. This honey skep probably formed part of the extensive breakfast service, comprising some eleven pieces, most of it made in Paul Storr's workshop and supplied to the Howe family by Rundell, Bridge and Rundell between 1800 and 1812.[1]

1 Sold Christie's, London, July 1, 1953, lot 139, now in the Museum of Fine Arts, Boston.

99

Wine cooler

Silver (sterling standard)

London, 1812/13

Maker's mark: Robert Garrard I (Grimwade, no. 2320)

Marks: Struck on rim with hallmarks (lion passant, leopard's head, date letter, duty mark) and with maker's mark

Description: Pail form, inverted truncated conical with bands of horizontal reeding, gadrooned rim and two D-form handles; engraved front and back with a coat of arms and crest within foliate mantling

H. 9 × W. 8 × D. 7⅝ in. (22.9 × 20.3 × 20 cm)
Weight: 44 oz. 10 dwt. (1390 g)

Heraldry: The arms are those of Alexander of Newtownlimavady and Londonderry, with those of Euen on an escutcheon of pretence.

The Alexander arms appear impaling those of an unknown family on a salver of 1733/34, mark of David Willaume II, in the Clark Art Institute, Williamstown, Massachusetts.[1]

Many of the client ledgers of Robert Garrard, whose business was the successor to the one started in Panton Street by George Wickes in the 1730s, survive but some ledgers are missing. "Mrs Alexander at Mr Dickson's Lisle Street" purchased a pint mug from the firm on December 14, 1812 and in 1816 Henry Alexander ordered a chased basket and a plated plateau, but the ledger which would have recorded any intervening purchases appears not to have survived.[2] In 1791 (see no. 91), Lord Weymouth had purchased from the firm "2 Plated Ice Pails with a bail across like a Common Pail".[3]

1 Wees, p. 441, no. 323.
2 AAD/1995/7/40 (VAM37) and AAD/1995/7/40 (VAM38).
3 AAD/1995/7/16 (VAM16).

100

Adjustable candlestick

Silver (sterling standard), fruitwood and silk

London, 1812/13

Maker's mark: Samuel Hennell (Grimwade, no. 2539)

Marks: Struck on base with hallmarks (lion passant, leopard's head, date letter, duty mark) and with maker's mark; the candle socket with lion passant and duty mark; the cylinder with lion passant, duty mark and maker's mark; the cap with lion passant and date letter; the slide with lion passant

Description: On circular base rising to a square stem with ball finial on which slides a candle socket with removable nozzle, held in place by a adjustable screw, the stem fitted with a vertical cylinder with hinged cap with vase-shaped finial, with adjustable slide to remove a folding green-silk circular shade

H. without shade: 10 × W. 5½ × D. 5 in. (25.5 × 14 × 12.7 cm)
Gross weight: 21 oz. 10 dwt. (671 g)

Heraldry: The monogram and coronet are those of the Earl of Essex.

Provenance: Probably George Capel-Coningsby, 5th Earl of Essex (1757–1839), by descent to Adela, Countess of Essex (d. 1922), Property from the Collections of the late Countess of Essex, Cassiobury Park, Watford, Herts, England, sale, Anderson Galleries, New York, December 10–16, 1922, lot 328; E. Swonnell (Silverware) Ltd., 1992

Exhibited: Temple Newsam House, Leeds, and Brighton Museum and Art Gallery, 1992

Published: Country House Lighting, p. 69, no. 46

99

The Domcha Collection

Adjustable candlesticks from the Georgian period are extremely rare. An adjustable arm with folding shade similar to this example was advertised in *Antique Collector*, August, 1987, p. 62, and an Irish example, made in Dublin about 1790, is in the Ticher Donation in the National Museum of Ireland.[1] A variation to this column with a sliding ejector for the fan was patented by Rose Jacob of Cockspur Street, London, in 1851. A virtually unique early version of a sliding candlestick is one of 1766/67, mark of Jonathan Alleine, in the Victoria & Albert Museum.[2] The Duke of Bedford purchased a "Chased Library Candlestick" from Garrard's in 1817, probably an adjustable one similar to this example.[3]

Samuel Hennell was one of a dynasty of silversmiths started by David Hennell, a specialist maker of salts, in the 1730s. The workshop of his cousin, Robert Hennell III, continued with his grandson, James Barclay Hennell, into the 1890s making highly finished large-scale works (nos. 105 and 107). Samuel's mark appears on an inkstand of 1813/14 fitted with a similar shaft with adjustable candle socket.[4]

As a young man, the 5th Earl of Essex had been a friend of the Prince of Wales and through the 1780s and 90s he moved in what was known as the Carlton House set. His first marriage, to the heiress Sarah Stephenson in 1786, was not a success and the couple lived apart until her death in 1838. Shortly afterwards, aged 80, he married Catherine Stephens, a comic actress famous for her unrivalled voice as a ballad singer. The earl himself was a noted cellist.

Numerous items in the 1922 sale cited above bore the same monogram and coronet; in addition, a coffee pot with the same monogram, of 1732/33, mark of John Edwards, was sold by Christie's, London, April 26, 1967 and is illustrated in Clayton, *History*, p. 149, no. 8.

1 Teahan, *Ticher*, p. 13, no. 4.
2 M.2:1-5-1918.
3 AAD/1995/7/37 (VAM36).
4 Sold Parke Bernet, New York, March 20, 1970, lot 230.

100

101

Toast-rack

Silver (sterling standard)

Sheffield, 1818/19

Maker's mark: Samuel Roberts, Jr., George Cadman and Co. (Jackson, p. 442, line 16)

Marks: Struck on frame with hallmarks (lion passant, combined town and date mark, duty mark) and with maker's mark

Description: Oblong, raised on four ball feet, formed of nine pointed arches, the centre applied with a scroll handle

H. 5¼ x W. 8⅝ x D. 3⅞ in. (12.3 x 21.9 x 9.9 cm)
Weight: 9 oz. (281 g)

The design of this toast-rack displays a transitional blend of styles. There is a hint of later Gothic revival in the pointed curves, while in the lower double arches there are remnants of earlier elliptical curves.

Roberts, Cadman and Company entered their first mark in Sheffield in 1786. The 1787 edition of *A Directory of Sheffield* lists them with an address in Eyre Street.

101

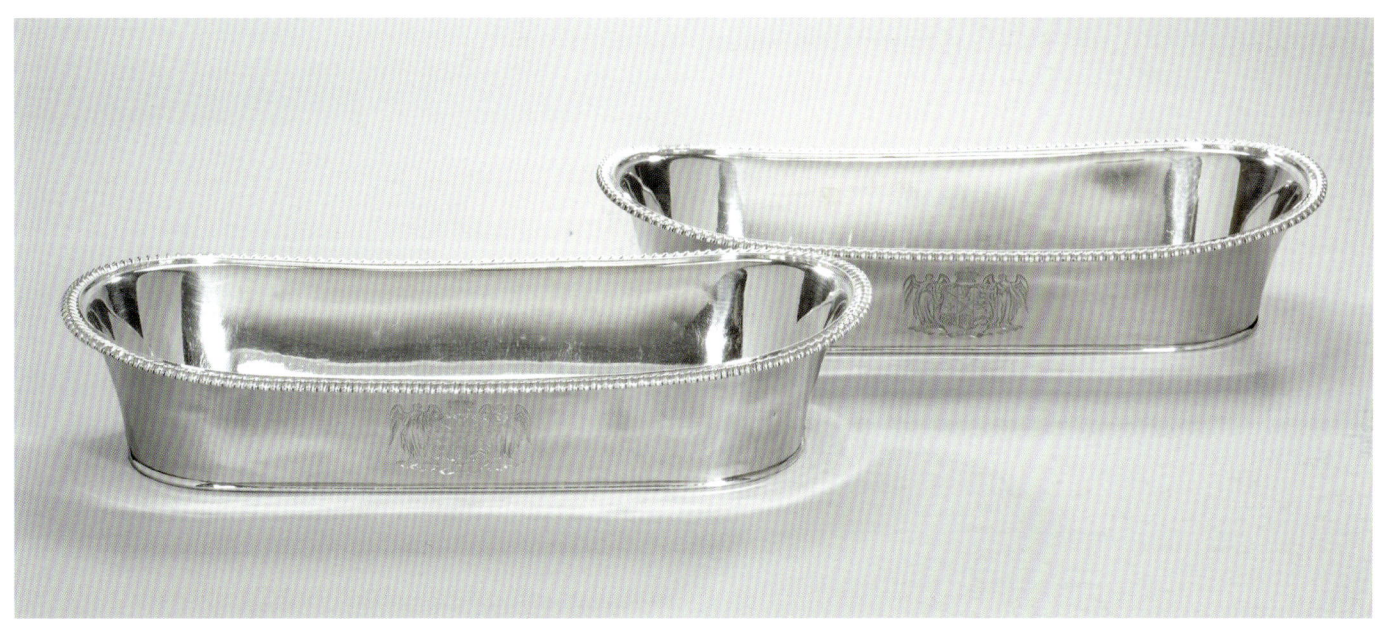

102

102

Pair of knife or pipe trays

Silver (sterling standard)

London, 1825/26 and 1827/28

Maker's mark: Robert Garrard II (Grimwade, no. 2322)

Marks: Struck on the side with hallmarks (lion passant, leopard's head, date letter, duty mark) and with maker's mark

Description: Straight-sided oblong with semicircular ends, gadrooned rims and everted sides, engraved on one side with a coat of arms, earl's coronet, motto and supporters and on the other side with a crest; the 1825/26 example stamped underneath *GARRARDS Panton Street LONDON*

H. 3¼ × W. 16¼ × D. 8 in. (8.3 × 41.2 × 20.3 cm)
Weight: 91 oz. 15 dwt. (2861 g)

Heraldry: The arms are those of Ward with many quarterings, as borne by John, 1st Earl of Dudley (1781–1833).

Provenance: John, 1st Earl of Dudley (1781–1833)

John Ward had a long parliamentary career culminating in his appointment as Secretary for Foreign Affairs in Canning's administration in 1827. In October of that year he was created Earl of Dudley. It was said that Caroline, Princess of Wales, complained of his eating habits which were likened to those of a hog, and Lady Charlotte Bury commented that he was "an unpleasant companion at table. Then his person looks so dirty; and he has such a sneer in his laugh, and is so

113

The Domcha Collection

103

impious, as well as grossly indecent in his conversation, that I cannot like this clever man". Vicary Gibbs recorded: "He is said, in a fit of absence of mind, to have, shortly before the battle of Navarino, directed a letter intended for the French ambassador to Prince Lieven, the ambassador from Russia. This, however, instead of working any mischief, was positively beneficial, being, fortunately, considered by the latter as a 'trap laid for him' and 'one of the cleverest *ruses* ever attempted to be played off'. Though a 'man of powerful talents, varied accomplishments', his eccentricities had always been so great that his aberration of mind during the last year of his life was not surprising." He died, without issue, in 1833.[1]

These trays form part of a large order of plate commissioned from Garrard's by Lord Dudley.[2] His purchases for the period from 1814 to 1819 are documented in their surviving *Gentleman's Ledger 3*, but the subsequent ledger which would have documented these objects appears not to have survived. Deep oblong trays from this period have traditionally been called "knife trays". Another possible function is for pipes: "An Inventorie of that Plate The Butler hath in his Charge at Knole", dated March 3, 1665/66, lists "one Long Dish for Tobbaco pipes".[3]

1 *Complete Peerage,* sub Dudley.
2 For example a pair of magnificent soup tureens, covers and stands of 1826/27, sold Sotheby's, London, June 26, 1975, lot 198.
3 West Kent Record Office/Sackville Papers/U269/E79.

103

Toasted-cheese dish

Silver (sterling standard)

Edinburgh, 1826

Maker's mark: JMc., for John McKay, James Mackie or James McKenzie (Jackson, p. 552, line 3)

Marks: Struck under base, on side, interior, inside cover and on liner with hallmarks (castle town mark, thistle, date letter, duty mark) and with maker's mark

Description: Rectangular with rounded corners and gadrooned rim, raised on four bun feet, with two foliate loop handles at each end, with internal hot-water compartment, the rear with hot-water cap, the slightly and partially domed hinged cover with acanthus-bud finial, the interior with removable liner; cover with coat of arms, crest and motto

H. 3½ × W. 12 × D. 7¾ in. (8.9 × 30.4 × 19.7 cm)
Weight: 57 oz. (1773 g)

Heraldry: The arms are those of Ramsay of Barnton, Edinburgh.

John McKay was admitted a freeman of the Edinburgh Goldsmiths' Company in 1793 and is recorded working in the High Street and North Bridge Street. There are, however, two other candidates for these initials, but McKay seems to be the most likely given his recorded addresses.[1]

1 Dalgleish and Maxwell, p. 40.

Geometry and the Silversmith

104

105

104

Stirrup cup

Silver (sterling standard), interior gilt

London, 1851/52

Maker's mark: John Samuel Hunt (Culme, no. 8350) for Hunt and Roskell

Marks: Struck under chin with hallmarks (lion passant, leopard's head, date letter, duty mark) and with maker's mark

Description: Realistically cast and chased as a terrier's head, with everted rim

H. 4½ × W. 6¼ × D. 3⅛ in. (11.4 × 15.8 × 7.9 cm)
Weight: 20 oz. 15 dwt. (650 g)

The popularity of drinking cups fashioned as animal heads dates back to antiquity. The custom was revived in the eighteenth century when fox-mask "stirrup cups" were made in both silver and ceramics. The Victorian era saw the repertory widened to include numerous breeds of dogs and other animals, executed, unlike the earlier fox cups which had been embossed out of sheet, in heavy cast silver.

Hunt and Roskell were the successors to a business started by Paul Storr in 1819 and, after the demise of Rundell, Bridge and Rundell in 1843, they were second only to Garrard's as the pre-eminent retailers of silver, luxury goods and jewellery.

105

Stirrup cup

Silver (sterling standard), interior gilt

London, 1880/81

Maker's mark: James Barclay Hennell (Culme, no. 8661) for Robert Hennell and Sons

Marks: Struck under chin with hallmarks (lion passant, leopard's head, date letter, duty mark) and with maker's mark

Description: Realistically cast and chased as a hound's head, with everted rim, the interior with suspension hook

H. 4 × W. 6⅛ × D. 4½ in. (10.1 × 15.5 × 11.4 cm)
Weight: 14 oz. 10 dwt. (452 g)

Provenance: The James Walker Collection of Silver and Vertu, sale, Christie's, South Kensington, July 13, 2006, lot 146

Hennell and Sons were a firm of manufacturing silversmiths started by David Hennell in 1735. They supplied high-quality work to many of the leading retailers of the time including Hunt and Roskell (see no. 104).[1]

1 Culme, p. 226.

The Domcha Collection

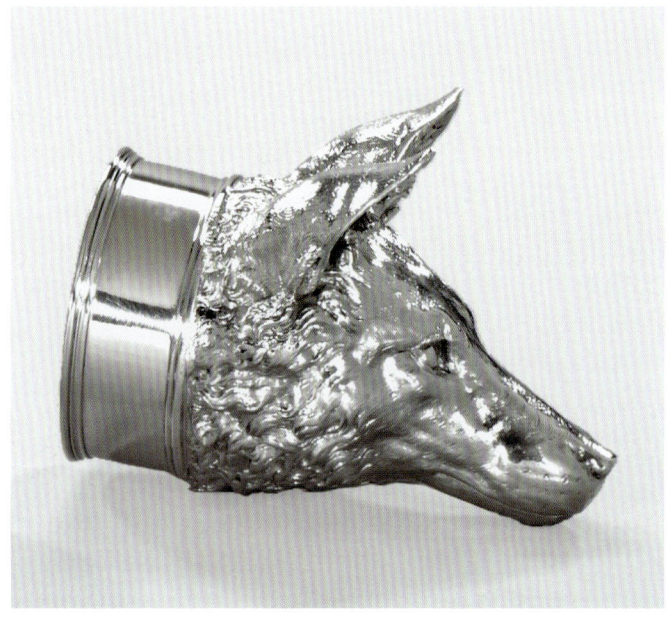

105

106

Stirrup cup

Silver (sterling standard), interior gilt

London, 1864/65

Maker's mark: John Samuel Hunt (Culme, no. 8350) for Hunt and Roskell

Marks: Struck on collar with hallmarks (lion passant, leopard's head, date letter, duty mark) and with maker's mark

Description: Realistically cast and chased as a fox head, with plain moulded collar, the collar stamped *2743*

H. 4 x W. 5 1/2 x D. 3 1/2 in. (10.1 x 14 x 8.9 cm)
Weight: 12 oz. 15 dwt. (396 g)

107

Punch, Judy and Toby cruet set

Silver (sterling standard), mustard pot with gilt interior

London, 1877/78; the dog 1875/76

Maker's mark: James Barclay Hennell (Culme, no. 8661) for Robert Hennell and Sons

Marks: Struck under bases with hallmarks (lion passant, leopard's head, date letter, duty mark) and with maker's mark, the covers with lion passant, duty mark and maker's mark

Description: Each piece realistically chased: a mustard pot in the form of Mr Punch, fitted with a spoon with leafy handle; a caster in the form of Mr Punch's wife Judy; a caster in the form of Toby the dog

Mr Punch:
H. 4 1/8 x W. 2 1/2 x D. 2 3/4 in. (10.5 x 6.3 x 7 cm)
Weight: 7 oz. 15 dwt. (240 g)

Judy:
H. 3 3/4 x W. 2 1/8 x D. 2 1/4 in. (9.5 x 5 4. x 5.7 cm)
Weight: 5 oz. 15 dwt. (178 g)

Toby the dog:
H. 3 1/4 x W. 1 3/4 x D. 2 1/8 in. (8.2 x 4.4 x 5.4 cm)
Weight: 4 oz. 10 dwt. (143 g)

This set is typical of the amusing novelty items popular on the dinner and tea table during the latter part of the Victorian era. This fashion could be seen as a revival of the whimsical objects produced during the middle years of the eighteenth century such as the cow creamer, no. 80.

Mr Punch arrived in London in the early years of the reign of Charles II, a period which saw the revival of theatrical performances. Samuel Pepys recorded in his diary on May 9, 1662 that he saw "… an Italian puppet play … which is very pretty, the best that I ever saw, and a great resort of gallants". The Punch and Judy show traces its roots back, however, to the Italian *commedia dell'arte* shows of the Middle Ages. The figure of Mr Punch is in fact the descendant of the Neapolitan character Pulcinella, which in time became anglicized to Punchinello. His wife's name was originally Joan but in the Victorian period it changed to Judy. The characters and the script became standardized, especially after the publication of John Payne Collier's transcription of *The Tragical Comedy or Comical Tragedy of Punch and Judy*, with illustrations by George Cruikshank, in 1828, which went through many subsequent editions.[1] Mr Punch himself was the inspiration for the satirical magazine *Punch* which was published from 1841 until 1992 and revived briefly from 1996.

The set is also struck with London Patent Office design registration marks for June 22, 1868. The problem of piracy of design was a perennial one for any manufacturer of luxury goods. It drove Rundell, Bridge and Rundell, the leading retailers of the first half of the nineteenth century, to set up their own design studio and workshops. From 1842, however, designs could be registered at the Patent Office and the lozenge-shaped mark, recording the class of object, the parcel number and the date the design was first registered, is often found not only on silverware but also on other metalwork and ceramics.

A similar cruet set, of 1878/79 and 1879/80, from the same workshop but lacking the mustard spoon, was sold Sotheby's, London, June 1, 2006, lot 67.

1 Stead, p. 85.

Geometry and the Silversmith

107

Glossary

Material

Alloy Base metal, usually copper, added to silver to yield a more hardwearing medium to make silver articles.

Assay The testing of silverware to ascertain the proportion of silver in the alloy (q.v.) used.

Britannia Standard The name given to a standard of silver alloy (q.v.) introduced for silverware on March 27, 1697 and in effect until June 1, 1720. It is over 95 per cent silver, some 2.5 per cent more than sterling standard, which it replaced, and the result is a much softer alloy. With the reintroduction of sterling alloy in 1720, Britannia continued as an optional higher standard.

Fruitwood Softwood of fruit-bearing trees such as the plum, apple, pear or cherry tree, used for handles and knobs on silverware.

Gold Metallic element (Au), characterized by its yellow colour. It is the most malleable and most highly prized of all metals.

Plate The term given to silverware (probably derived from the Spanish word for silver, *plata*). In recent times, it has sometimes been used to refer to silver-plated articles.

Silver Metallic element (Ag) that is ductile and malleable, generally alloyed with copper to increase its hardness.

Standard The elemental composition of silver alloy; in England the two standards used have been Britannia (q.v.) and sterling (q.v.).

Sterling Silver alloy (q.v.) used as the legal standard since the Middle Ages, except for a brief period between 1697 and 1720 when the higher, Britannia, standard was used. In 12 troy ounces of metal, 11 $^{1}/_{10}$ ounces are pure silver. This is the equivalent of 92.5 per cent pure silver in the alloy.

Techniques

Burnishing Process of rubbing the surface of silver to produce a bright, smooth finish; stone tools were often used.

Casting Technique by which molten metal is poured into a mould. Lost-wax casting involves a wax model that is encased in clay or plaster and then burned out, leaving a mould. Sand-casting was also frequently used for candlesticks and other components. Here a model is made in wood, lead or beeswax and pressed into a bed of sand. The molten silver is then poured into the impression.

Chasing Process of embossing the surface of an object by placing it against a bed of pitch and striking the front of it with punches of various shapes, resulting in a three-dimensional effect.

Engraving Surface decoration done by using hand-held burins, or gravers, to incise a small line. Unlike chasing, which only moves the metal, engraving removes a small amount of it.

Gilding Gold-plating of silver, in which gold was melted in a crucible with mercury and the resulting paste was brushed over the surface of the silver. The mercury evaporated, leaving the gold, which was then burnished to a high polish. This process, which was extremely dangerous to the participants, was replaced by electro-gilding in the nineteenth century.

Raising Highly skilled process by which a piece of flat sheet silver is hammered over iron or wooden stakes to form the body of a vessel. Periodic "annealing," in which the metal is heated to a dull red colour and then plunged in cold water, thereby relieving the stresses that have built up in the crystalline structure of the metal, is necessary to prevent the metal from splitting.

Form and Decoration

Baluster A bellied form popular from the end of the seventeenth century onwards for silver vessels like casters, coffee pots and candlestick stems, from the French *balustre*, which derives from the Greek *balaustion*, a wild pomegranate flower, so-named because it resembles the curving calyx tube of the flower.

Baroque A style incorporating classical motifs and dynamic surfaces creating a feeling of movement, and prevalent in European decorative arts of the seventeenth and early eighteenth centuries.

Cartouche Derived from parchment scrolls, it is a tablet-form motif, usually elliptical, containing a coat of arms or monogram and enclosed by an elaborate frame.

Ellipse A plane closed curve (in popular language a regular oval) in which the sum of the distances of any point from the two foci is constant. "It is frequently but erroneously called an oval" (John Carroll, *Practical Geometry for Art Students*, London, 1881).

In Cartesian coordinates the simplest form of the equation for a true ellipse is expressed in terms of x and y both raised to the power of 2. This may be regarded as a particular case within a family known as Lamé curves where the power of both x and y may be any value n greater than zero. A subellipse is a Lamé curve where n is less than 2 (see serving trowel, no. 75, where n appears to be approximately 1.7). A superellipse is a Lamé curve where n is greater than 2. As n is increased a Lamé curve becomes ever more rectangular. Tray, no. 46, may thus perhaps be a superellipse.

It is not known how subellipses and superellipses might have been generated in the eighteenth century, but it is nevertheless interesting that the mathematics of Gabriel Lamé (1795–1870) confirms aesthetically pleasing curves as used by silversmiths.

See N.T. Gridgeman, "Lamé ovals", *The Mathematical Gazette*, vol. 54, no. 387, February, 1970, pp. 31–7. See also J. Allard, "Notes on Pseudo-Rectangles", *Mathematics Magazine*, vol. 38, no. 2, March, 1965, pp. 61–4.

Gadrooning Ornament consisting of convex slightly curved lobes which was very popular as an applied edge to silver objects from the early eighteenth century onwards. In contemporary accounts, it is often referred to as "knurling."

Hexagon A six-sided figure.

Oblong Rectangle (q.v.) with the adjacent sides of uneven length.

Octagon An eight-sided figure.

Octofoil An eight-lobed figure.

Polygon A many-sided figure.

Rectangle A four-sided figure in which the opposing sides are parallel and all angles are right angles.

Patera, paterae A circular or elliptical ornament formed of leaves or petals.

Reeding A moulding resembling a bundle of reeds.

Rococo A nineteenth-century word used to describe the asymmetrical curves and naturalism of the 1730s and 1740s, the final flowering of the baroque. The main ingredient of rococo is *rocaille*, broken or foliate scrolls, and naturalistically depicted flowers, leaves and fauna.

Subellipse See *ellipse*.

Superellipse See *ellipse*.

Trencher Originally used to refer to the stale slice of bread on which food was served to the humbler sort during the Middle Ages; later it came to refer to a place setting, as in trencher salt or trencher plate.

Heraldry and Rank

Achievement The full armorial display of coat of arms (q.v.), crest (q.v.), supporters (q.v.) and motto, often contained in elaborate mantling of a cartouche.

Badge Symbol used by the head of certain great families since the Middle Ages. Not to be confused with a crest (q.v.). It has no heraldic significance.

Baron The fifth degree of the peerage.

Baronet A hereditary knight (q.v.), often abbreviated Bt, or Bart.

Blazon A description of a coat of arms using heraldic terms.

Cadency, Mark of Symbol applied to a coat of arms to denote a son of the bearer.

Coat of arms Process of identifying an individual with a decorated shield developed in the Middle Ages and by the seventeenth century the right to bear a coat of arms was avidly sought as a symbol of gentility. The practice of engraving or applying arms on silverware as identification blossomed during the eighteenth century, and nowadays often makes the identification of the original owners possible. A coat of arms is sometimes erroneously referred to as a "crest" (q.v.).

College of Arms Body which governs the use of heraldry in England.

Coronet Circlet worn by a peer (q.v.), or peeress, to denote their rank.

Countess Wife of an earl.

Crest Heraldic symbol originally worn on the helmet as identification when the visor was closed. It appears above a coat of arms as part of armorials and sometimes appears engraved on silver separately from the shield. A crest can pertain to a number of families, making precise identification difficult if it appears alone without a shield, initials or a coronet of rank.

Duke The highest rank of the peerage.

Earl The third degree of the peerage.

Escutcheon A shield.

Escutcheon of pretence If a man marries an heiress (a daughter with no brothers), he can display her father's arms on a small shield (or escutcheon) superimposed on his own coat of arms, rather than impaling them (q.v.).

Impalement A man can "impale" his own coat of arms with those of his wife's father, by dividing the shield down the centre and displaying his own on the left and his wife's on the right.

Knight A member of an order of chivalry, which confers the title of Sir.

Lozenge Coat of arms depicted in a diamond-shaped shield, denoting arms borne by a spinster or widow or a peeress in her own right.

Lyon Office Body which governs the use of heraldry in Scotland, the English equivalent being the College of Arms (q.v.).

Mantling Originally a long robe worn over armour which in heraldry forms the decoration behind a shield.

Marquess The second degree of the peerage.

Peer A nobleman bearing one of the titles of rank.

Peeress A noblewomen, wife of a nobleman.

Pretence see escutcheon of pretence.

Quarterly Shield divided into four quarters or more than four sections.

Supporters The heraldic beasts or human figures which flank a coat of arms in a full armorial achievement (q.v.).

Tinctures The colours of the components of a coat of arms. As colour cannot be depicted in engraving, a system of hatching different backgrounds, each one denoting a colour, evolved in the seventeenth century.

Viscount The fourth degree of the peerage.

Customers and the Trade

Apprentice Fourteen-year-old boy "bound" to a Master, or Freeman, to learn the trade, living with his family and working in his business. It was usual for a premium to be paid for this by the boy's parents. Occasionally, owing to the death or change of circumstance of a Master, an apprentice would be "turned over" to another Master. After the completion of his seven-year apprenticeship the boy could be admitted a Freeman (q.v.) of the Goldsmiths' Company (q.v.), or another livery company, which would enable him, as a Freeman of the City of London, to carry on a trade within its jurisdiction. Apprenticeship rules in other towns were essentially the same.

Edict of Nantes Henri IV's edict granting religious freedoms to the Huguenots, which was revoked by Louis XIV in 1685, causing a huge exodus of refugees from France.

Freeman Member of a livery company (trade guild). Membership of one of the London guilds brought with it the Freedom of the City of London, and the ability to pursue a trade within its jurisdiction. Admission to the Freedom of the Goldsmiths' Company was by one of three ways: Patrimony, by reason of applicant's father having been admitted a Freeman before, Servitude, by serving a seven-year apprenticeship, and Redemption, by payment of a fee.

Goldsmiths' Company (The Worshipful Company of Goldsmiths) Trade guild of the gold- and silversmiths of London, incorporated by a charter from King Edward III in 1327. It continues to oversee the regulation of the manufacturing trade and its Assay Office continues to test the alloy of new silverware. The term goldsmiths' company is also used to describe guilds of other cities or towns.

Huguenot Name given to French Protestants of the sixteenth and seventeenth centuries, usually thought to derive from the Dutch *eedgenot* or the Swiss German *eidgenoss* meaning confederate, assimilated with the name of a Genevan burgo-master, Besançon Hugues.

Journeyman Craftsman who, having completed his apprenticeship, was employed by a silversmith (the word comes from the French *journée* meaning a day's duration: a journeyman was hired and paid by the day). Journeymen were distinct from silversmiths who had registered a maker's mark at Goldsmiths' Hall and were in business on their own account.

Largeworker In the early eighteenth century, makers' marks were recorded in two books at Goldsmiths' Hall, one for "largeworkers", i.e., makers of full-scale articles and one for "smallworkers", i.e., makers of small items and components like the mounts of boxes.

MP Abbreviation for Member of Parliament.

Smallworker *See* Largeworker.

Marks

Britannia Stamp of the seated figure of Britannia to denote Britannia standard silver (i.e., 958/1000 alloy), in use between 1697 and 1720.

Castle stamp Hallmark denoting silver made in Edinburgh, used from 1485 onwards.

Crown stamp Hallmark denoting silver made in Sheffield, used from 1773 to the present day.

Crowned harp stamp Hallmark denoting silver made in Dublin, used from 1637 to the present day.

Date letter Official, or hall-, mark, struck on silver to denote the year in which the object was assayed. Formed of a letter of the alphabet, it was usually changed in May each year.

Hallmarks Official stamps, or marks, struck on finished silverware by the wardens of the London Goldsmiths' Company, or by the guild of another city or town, to signify that the silver was of the legal standard of alloy. Not to be confused with makers' marks (q.v.), which are not official stamps.

Hibernia stamp Hallmark used in Dublin from 1730 onwards. The mark was originally used to denote payment of the duty on manufactured gold and silver, but after 1807, when an Act of Parliament immediately following the Union established a monarch's-head duty mark (as used by the assay offices in England and Scotland), the Hibernia mark continued to be used as a "town mark" for Dublin.

Leopard's head stamp Hallmark denoting silver made in London, used from the Middle Ages to the present day, with the exception of the period 1697–1720 when it was replaced with the lion's head erased (q.v.).

Lion's head erased stamp Hallmark denoting silver assayed in London between 1697 and 1720. "Erased", a heraldic term, refers to the way in which the head is cut off with a jagged line.

Lion passant stamp Hallmark used in England to denote sterling standard silver, depicting a lion with his right (dexter) foreleg raised as if walking.

Maker's mark Also known as sponsor's mark. A mark registered with the Goldsmiths' Company by manufacturers or retailers of silverware who brought the article in for assaying and hallmarking.

Scratch weight Weight of a piece of silver expressed in ounces and pennyweights, engraved or scratched on the reverse or under the base of an object by the silversmith or valuer commonly applied in the seventeenth and eighteenth centuries for inventory purposes.

Three-tower stamp Hallmark denoting silver assayed in Newcastle-upon-Tyne, used from the beginning of the eighteenth century until 1884.

Bibliography

Alcorn, *Lamerie*
Ellenor Alcorn, *Beyond the Maker's Mark: Paul de Lamerie Silver in the Cahn Collection*, Cambridge, 2006

Alcorn, *MFA I*
Ellenor Alcorn, *English Silver in the Museum of Fine Arts, Boston*, vol. I, *Silver before 1697*, Boston, 1993

Alcorn, *MFA II*
Ellenor Alcorn, *English Silver in the Museum of Fine Arts, Boston*, vol. II, *Silver from 1697*, Boston, 2000

Bannister, "Jenkins"
Judith Bannister, "The Master Craftsman", *Proceedings of the Society of Silver Collectors*, vol. 2, no. 11, 1976, pp. 187–93

Barr
Elaine Barr, *George Wickes, Royal Goldsmith 1698–1761*, London, 1980

Bennett
Douglas Bennett, *Collecting Irish Silver*, London, 1984

Bennett, *Georgian*
Douglas Bennett, *Irish Georgian Silver*, London, 1972

Bennett, *Trinity*
Douglas Bennett, *The Silver Collection, Trinity College Dublin*, Dublin, 1988

Blair
Claude Blair, *The Goldsmith and the Grape*, exh. cat., Goldsmiths' Hall, London, 1983

Brett
Vanessa Brett, *The Sotheby's Directory of Silver, 1600–1940*, London, 1986

Brett, *Dinner*
Gerard Brett, *Dinner is Served: A History of Dining in England 1400–1900*, London, 1968

Burlington
J. Starkie Gardner (ed.), *Collection of Silversmiths' Work of European Origin*, exh. cat., Burlington Fine Arts Club, London, 1901

Butler, *Albert*
Robin Butler, *The Albert Collection: Five Hundred Years of British and European Silver*, London, 2004

Butler, *Wine*
Robin Butler, *The Book of Wine Antiques*, Woodbridge, 1986

Cameron
Peter Cameron, "Henry Jernegan, the Kandlers and the client who changed his mind", *The Silver Society Journal*, vol. 8, 1996, pp. 487–501

Cassidy-Geiger, "Sugar and silver"
Maureen Cassidy-Geiger, "Sugar and silver into porcelain: The conditorei and court dining in Dresden under Augustus III", *Silver Studies, The Journal of the Silver Society*, vol. 22, 2007, pp. 152–4

Clayton, *Dictionary*
Michael Clayton, *The Collector's Dictionary of Silver and Gold of Great Britain and North America*, rev. edn., Woodbridge, 1985

Clayton, *History*
Michael Clayton, *Christie's Pictorial History of English and American Silver*, Oxford, 1985

Complete Peerage
George Edward Cockayne, *The Complete Peerage of England, Scotland, Ireland, Great Britain and the United Kingdom*, London, 1887–98

Country House Lighting
Country House Lighting, exh. cat., Temple Newsam, Leeds, 1992

Culme
John Culme, *The Directory of Gold & Silversmiths, Jewellers & Allied Traders, 1838–1914*, Woodbridge, 1987

Dalgleish and Maxwell
George Dalgleish and Stuart Maxwell, *The Lovable Craft 1687–1987: An Exhibition to celebrate the 300th anniversary of the Royal Charter of the Incorporation of Goldsmiths of the City of Edinburgh*, exh. cat., Royal Museum of Scotland, Edinburgh, 1987

Dalgleish and Steuart Fothringham
George Dalgleish and Henry Steuart Fothringham, *Silver Made in Scotland*, exh. cat., National Museums Scotland, 2008

Davis
John D. Davis, *English Silver at Williamsburg*, Williamsburg, 1976

Davis, *Nutmegs*
J. Davis, *The Robert and Meredith Green Collection of Silver Nutmeg Graters*, Williamsburg, 2002

Delamer and O'Brien
Ida Delamer and Conor O'Brien, "Dublin hallmarks: a reappraisal of the date letters used 1638–1736," *The Silver Society Journal*, no. 11, 1999, pp. 158–67

Delieb
Eric Delieb, *Investing in Silver*, London, 1967

Dixon
Stanley C. Dixon, *English Decorated Trays*, London, 1964

Drummond
J.C. Drummond and Anne Wilbraham, *The Englishman's Food, Five Centuries of English Diet*, rev. edn., London, 1957

Dunbar
John G. Dunbar, *The Historic Architecture of Scotland*, London, 1966

Edwards
A.C. Edwards, *The Account Books of Benjamin Mildmay, Earl Fitzwalter*, London, 1977

Gifford
John Gifford, *William Adam 1689–1748, a Life and Times of Scotland's Universal Architect*, Edinburgh, 1989

Gill
Margaret A.V. Gill, *A Directory of Newcastle Goldsmiths*, Newcastle, 1976

Glanville, "Boughton"
  Philippa Glanville, "Boughton Silver", in Tessa Murdoch, ed., *Boughton House, the English Versailles*, London, 1992, pp. 151–7

Glanville, *Tudor and Early Stuart*
  Philippa Glanville, *Silver in Tudor and Early Stuart England*, London, 1990

Godfrey
  Honor Godfrey, *The Colman Collection of Silver Mustard Pots*, Norwich, 1979

Grimwade
  Arthur G. Grimwade, *London Goldsmiths 1697–1837, Their Marks and Lives*, rev. edn., London, 1990

Grimwade, "Anglo-Jewish Silver"
  Arthur G. Grimwade, "Anglo-Jewish Silver", *The Transactions of the Jewish Historical Society of England*, vol. XVIII, 1953, pp. 113–25

Grimwade, "Bills"
  Arthur G. Grimwade, "Paul de Lamerie's bills: A comparative study of the major surviving plate accounts," *The Silver Society Journal*, no. 10, 1998, pp. 60–61

Grimwade, "Master"
  Arthur G. Grimwade, "The Master of George Vertue," *Apollo*, vol. 127, no. 312, 1988, pp. 83–9

Grimwade, *Queen's*
  Arthur G. Grimwade, *The Queen's Silver*, London, 1953

Grimwade, "Tankards"
  Arthur G. Grimwade, "English Silver Tankards", *Apollo*, December, 1953

Gubbins
  Martin Gubbins, *York Assay Office & Silversmiths, 1776–1857*, York, 1983

Hackenbroch
  Yvonne Hackenbroch, *English and Other Silver in the Irwin Untermyer Collection*, rev. edn. New York, 1969

Hare
  Susan Hare (ed.), *Paul de Lamerie: At the Sign of The Golden Ball. An Exhibition of the Work of England's Master Silversmith (1688–1751)*, exh. cat., Goldsmiths' Hall, London, 1990

Hartop, "Continental"
  Christopher Hartop, "Continental Silver in English Churches", T. Schroder, ed., *Treasures of the Church*, exh. cat., Goldsmiths' Hall, London, 2008, pp. 116–25

Hartop, "Elizabethan"
  Christopher Hartop, "An Elizabethan Rarity", *Christie's Review of the Season, 1986*, London, 1987, pp. 306–7

Hartop, "Engraving"
  Christopher Hartop, "Engraving on English Silver, 1680–1760," *The Magazine Antiques*, vol. CLI, no. 2, February, 1997, pp. 339–49

Hartop, *Fogg*
  Christopher Hartop, *British and Irish Silver in the Fogg Art Museum, Harvard University Art Museums*, Cambridge, Massachusetts, 2007

Hartop, *Huguenot*
  Christopher Hartop, *The Huguenot Legacy: English Silver, 1680–1760, from the Alan and Simone Hartman Collection*, London, 1996

Hartop, "Norwich"
  Christopher Hartop, "Norwich goldsmiths 1700–1800", *Silver Studies, the Journal of the Silver Society*, no. 21, 2006, pp. 73–86

Hartop, "Patrons and Consumers"
  Christopher Hartop, "Patrons and consumers: buying silver in eighteenth-century London", *Rococo Silver in England and Its Colonies*, London, 2006

Hartop, *Rundell*
  Christopher Hartop, *Royal Goldsmiths: The Art of Rundell & Bridge 1797–1843*, Cambridge, 2005

Hayward
  J.F. Hayward, *Huguenot Silver in England, 1688–1727*, London, 1959

Heal
  Ambrose Heal, *The London Goldsmiths 1200–1800: A Record of the Names and Addresses of the Craftsmen, their Shop-signs and Trade-cards*, Newton Abbot, 1972

Heilbron
  J.L. Heilbron, *Geometry Civilized: History, Culture and Technique*, Oxford, 1998

Helft
  Jacques Helft, *Le Poinçon des provinces françaises*, Paris, 1985

Holland
  Margaret Holland, *Old Country Silver*, Newton Abbot, 1971

How, *Notes 1946–47*
  G.E.P. How, *Notes on Antique Silver, 1946–47*, London, 1947

Ivins
  William M. Ivins, *Art & Geometry, a Study in Space Intuitions*, New York, 1946

Jackson
  Ian Pickford (ed.), *Jackson's Silver and Gold Marks of England, Scotland and Ireland*, rev. edn., Woodbridge, 1989

Jackson, 1921
  Sir Charles James Jackson, *English Goldsmiths and Their Marks*, London, 1921

Jackson, *English Plate*
  Charles James Jackson, *An Illustrated History of English Plate Ecclesiastical and Secular …*, London, 1911

Jones, *Farrer*
  E. Alfred Jones, *Catalogue of the Collection of Old Plate of William Francis Farrer at No. 7, St. James's Square, London*, London, 1924

Kent, *Spoonmakers*
  Timothy Kent, *London Silver Spoonmakers, 1500 to 1697*, London, 1981

Lomax
  James Lomax, *British Silver at Temple Newsam and Lotherton Hall*, Leeds, 1992

Lomax, "Jewel House"
: James Lomax, "Royalty and silver: the role of the Jewel House in the eighteenth century", *The Silver Society Journal*, no. 11, 1999, pp. 133–140

Lomax and Rothwell
: James Lomax and James Rothwell, *Country House Silver from Dunham Massey*, London, 2006

McNab
: Jessie McNab, *Silver*, New York, 1981

Micio
: Paul Micio, "Fantastic piercework by the unknown 'Stencil Master'", *Apollo*, vol. CLVI, no. 491 (New Series), January, 2003, pp. 22–31

Miles
: Elizabeth Miles, *The English Silver Nutmeg Grater, a Collection of Fifty Examples from 1693 to 1816* (The Miles Collection), Cleveland, 1966

Murdoch, "Harpies"
: Tessa Murdoch, "Harpies and Hunting Scenes: Paul Crespin, Huguenot Goldsmith", *Country Life*, August 29, 1985

Murdoch, *Noble*
: Tessa Murdoch, ed., *Noble Households: Eighteenth-Century Inventories of Great English Houses*, Cambridge, 2006

Murray
: Hugh Murray, *Directory of York Goldsmiths, Silversmiths & Associated Craftsmen*, York, 1998

Old English Plate, 1929
: *Loan Exhibition of Old English Plate*, exh. cat., 25 Park Lane, London, 1929

Oxford Plate
: *Catalogue of a Loan Exhibition of Silver Plate belonging to the Colleges of the University of Oxford*, exh. cat., Ashmolean Museum, Oxford, 1928

Papworth
: John W. Papworth, *Ordinary of British Armorials*, London, 1874

Pedoe
: Dan Pedoe, *Geometry and the Liberal Arts*, Harmondsworth, 1976

Phillips
: Phillip A.S. Phillips, *Paul de Lamerie, Citizen and Goldsmith of London: A Study of His Life and Work, A.D. 1688–1751*, London, 1935

Pijzel-Dommisse
: Jet Pijzel-Dommisse, *Haags goud en zilver: Edelsmeedkunst uit de Hofstad*, The Hague, 2005

Preston
: Arthur E. Preston, *The Abingdon Corporation Plate*, Oxford, 1958

Queen Charlotte, 1929
: *Queen Charlotte's Loan Exhibition of Old Silver*, exh. cat., Seaford House, Belgrave Square, London, 1929

Rabinovitch
: Benton Seymour Rabinovitch, *Antique Silver Servers for the Table*, Concord, Massachusetts, 1991

Schroder, *National Trust*
: Timothy Schroder, *The National Trust Book of English Domestic Silver: 1500–1900*, Harmondsworth, 1988

Sinsteden, "Assay Records"
: Thomas Sinsteden, "Four selected assay records of the Dublin Goldsmiths' Company", *The Silver Society Journal*, no. 11, 1999, pp. 143–57

Sinsteden, "Assay Records 2"
: Thomas Sinsteden, "Surviving Dublin assay records", *Silver Studies, the Journal of the Silver Society*, no. 16, 2004, pp. 87–102

Sitwell
: Hervey Degge Wilmot Sitwell, "The Jewel House and the Royal Goldsmiths," *Archaeological Journal*, vol. 75, 1948, pp. 131–55

Snodin
: Michael Snodin, *English Silver Spoons*, London, rev. edn., 1982

Stead
: Philip John Stead, *Mr. Punch*, London, 1950

Sweeney
: Tony Sweeney, *Irish Stuart Silver*, Dublin, 1995

Tayler
: Alistair and Henrietta Tayler, *The Book of the Duffs*, 2 vols., Edinburgh, 1914

Teahan
: John Teahan, *Irish Silver from the Seventeenth to the Nineteenth Century*, exh. cat., Smithsonian Institution, Washington, D.C., 1982

Teahan, *Ticher*
: John Teahan, *The Dr. Kurt Ticher Donation of Irish Silver to the National Museum of Ireland*, Dublin, n.d.

Thornton
: Peter Thornton, *Seventeenth-Century Interior Decoration in England, France and Holland*, New Haven and London, 1978

Voet and van Gelder
: Elias Voet and H.E. van Gelder, *Merken van Haagsche goud- en zilversmeden, Haagsche goud- en zilversmeden uit de XVIe en XVIIIe eeuw*, The Hague, 1941

Wark
: Robert R. Wark, *British Silver in the Huntington Collection*, San Marino, 1978

Watney and Babbidge
: Bernard M. Watney and Homer D. Babbidge, *Corkscrews for Collectors*, London, 1981

Wees
: Beth Carver Wees, *English, Irish & Scottish Silver at the Sterling and Francine Clark Art Institute*, New York, 1997

Wilding
: Peter Wilding, *An Introduction to English Silver*, London, 1950

Picture credits

By permission of the British Library, fig. 2

Syndics of Cambridge University Library, fig. 8 and p. 55, upper right

Carnegie Museum of Art, Pittsburgh, p. 96, lower left

Christie's Images Ltd., fig. 9 and p. 96, upper right

Reproduced by courtesy of Essex Record Office, p. 87

© President and Fellows of Harvard College, *Two-Handled Cup and Cover*, 1655–1656, maker's mark: WH, mullet above, pellet in annulet below, silver, 7⅞ × 8⅛ × 5½ in. (20 × 20.64 × 13.97 cm), weight: 25 oz. 11 dwt. (800 g), Harvard Art Museum, Fogg Art Museum, Bequest of Archibald A. Hutchinson, Esq., 1949.114.42.A-B, Photo: Junius Beebe, fig. 6

Cincinnati Art Museum, The Folgers Coffee Silver Collection, Gift of the Procter & Gamble Company, fig. 7

© National Portrait Gallery, London, p. 77, lower right

Photograph courtesy Peabody Essex Museum, E82766.AB Teapot, c.1679, fig. 13

© 1990 Photo SCALA, Florence/Gabinetto dei Disegni et delle Stampe degli Uffizi, Florence, courtesy of the Ministero Beni e Att. Culturali, fig. 5

The Worshipful Company of Goldsmiths, London, facing the Foreword and fig. 4

Index

Catalogue-entry numbers are given for items in the Domcha Collection as well as for their makers, heraldry, marks and provenance. These numbers are shown in **boldface**. Page numbers are given for illustrations from sources other than the Domcha Collection and are shown in *italic*; all other page references are given in roman. Some technical terms are defined in the glossary but references to them occurring elsewhere in the book are given in the index.

Affre I, Jean
    dish, **83**
Affre, Étienne, 97
Ancaster, 2nd Duke of.
    See Bertie, Peregrine
apple corer, **65**
Archer, Andrew
    spoon, strainer, **41**
Arfe, Juan de
    De Varia Commensuración, 18, *18*
argyll
    Carter, John, **87**
Arnett, Hugh, 85

Barnard I, Edward, & Emes, Rebecca
    honey skep, **98**
Barnard I, John
    candlesticks, **14**
Barry, William (poss.), **48**
Bateman, Peter & Ann
    serving spoons and a fork, **96**
Bath, 1st Marquess of.
    See Thynne, Thomas, 1st Marquess of Bath
Batty II, Francis
    jug, hot-milk, **20**
beakers
    Hall I, William (poss.), **3**
    Harrison I, William (poss.), **3**
    Pocock, Edward, **71**
    Wickes, George, **78** (nesting)
Beckford, William, 107
Beckwith, Ambrose, 101
beer bowls, 28
beer jug
    Farren, Thomas, **45**
Bellassye, William
    caster or wig duster, **30**
Bertie, Peregrine, 2nd Duke of Ancaster, 67
Bird, Joseph
    tapersticks, **27**

Bolton, Thomas
    salts, trencher, **13**
Böttger, Johann Friedrich, 20
bowl, two-handled
    Partis I, Thomas, **54**
Braford, Benjamin, 48
Bute, 4th Earl of.
    See Stuart, John, 4th Earl of Bute
Buteux, Abraham, 89

cake basket
    Crespin, Paul, **67**
candlesticks.
    See also tapersticks
    Barnard I, John, **14**
    Hennell, Samuel, **100** (adjustable)
    Parr I, Thomas, **35**
Capel-Coningsby, George, 5th Earl of Essex, 112
Carter, John
    argyll, **87**
casserole and cover
    Wakelin, John, & Tayler, William, **91**
casters, **17**, **107**
    Bellassye, William, **30**
    Chartier, John, **33**
    Jones, George Greenhill, **31**
    Jones I, John, **32**
Chartier, John
    casters, **33**
    sugar box, **28**
Chawner, Henry
    dishes, meat, **92**
cheese stand
    Hougham, Solomon, **95**
Chinese export porcelain and stoneware, 19–20
chocolate pot
    Rotheram, Caleb, **59**
coffee pots
    Edwards II, John, **53**
    Tearle, Thomas, **56**
    White, John, **55**
    Wickes, George, **14**, *15*
Coles, Lawrence, 45
condiment pots
    Cripps, William (prob.), **84**
Cooper I, Matthew, 50
    waiter, **57**
coral, **9**
corkscrew with nutmeg grater
    Parker, William, **97**
Courtauld, Augustine, 82, 85
    salver, *16*
cow creamer
    Schuppe, John, **80**
Craig, John
    inkstand, **85**

Geometry and the Silversmith

cream jugs
    Schuppe, John, **80**
    Vincent, Edward, **16**
    Wastell, Samuel, **62**
creamers. *See* cream jugs, *and* cow creamer
Crespell I, Sebastian, & Crespell, James
    saucepan and cover, **88**
Crespin, Paul
    cake basket, **67**
Cripps, William (prob.)
    condiment pots, **84**
cruet set
    Hennell, James Barclay, **107**
cup, two-handled, *13*
Curzon, Richard, 1st Earl Howe, 109

Dell, Samuel (poss.)
    tumbler cup, **11**
design
    Asian influence on, 19–20
Dicken, Arthur
    teapot, **44**
dishes, 1
    Affre I, Jean, **83**
    Lamerie, Paul de, **73**
    fluted
        Willaume I, David, **38**
        Willaume II, David, **60**
        Kandler, Frederick, **82**
            (with covers)
    meat
        Chawner, Henry, **92**
    sallet, 76–7, 95
    strawberry, 77
    toasted-cheese
        McKay, John (prob.), **103**
dredger. *See* kitchen peppers
Dudley, 1st Earl of. *See* Ward, John
Duff, William, 1st Earl Fife, 53, 55
Dürer, Albrecht, 12
Dutch silversmiths
    Havelaar, Adrian
        salver, **47**
    Koop, Johannes
        spoon with marrow spoon, **24**
Dwight, John, 20
Dymick, Thomas, 34

Edgar, Devereux, 59
Edgcumbe, Sir Richard, 30
Edwards II, John
    coffee pot, **53**
egg frame
    Wilme I, John (prob.), **79**

Emes, Rebecca, & Barnard I, Edward
    honey skep, **98**
engravers of silver
    Gentot, Blaise, 42
    Rollos, John, 42
Essex, 5th Earl of. *See* Capel-Coningsby, George
Euclid, 11, 12, 14–16, 19
    Elements of Geometry, 15, *16*

Farren, Thomas
    beer jug, **45**
Fawdery, John, 48
Fawdery, William
    teapot, **49**
Feline, Edward
    salver, **72**
Feline, Magdalen, 85
Fife, 1st Earl. *See* Duff, William
Fitzgerald, James, 20th Earl of Kildare, 91
Fitzwalter, 1st Earl. *See* Mildmay, Benjamin
flasks
    Meale, George, **39**
    Wilks, James (prob.), **40**
Fogelberg, Andrew, 107
fork and pair of serving spoons
    Bateman, Peter & Ann, **96**
Fountayne, John, Dean of York, 81
Francis, Benjamin (poss.)
    tankard, **2**
French silversmiths
    Affre I, Jean
        dish, **83**
    Affre, Étienne, 97
funnel
    Pantin I, Simon, **70**

Gamon, John
    wine-bottle stand, **69**
Garrard I, Robert
    wine cooler, **99**
Garrard I, Robert, & Wakelin, John
    pail, **93**
Garrard II, Robert
    trays, knife or pipe, **102**
Garthorne, Francis
    plates, dinner, **12**
Gentot, Blaise, 42
"geometric style", 14
geometrical shapes
    cone
        funnel
            Pantin I, Simon, **70**
        truncated
            chocolate pot
                Rotheram, Caleb, **59**

cone, truncated *cont'd*
    coffee pots
        Tearle, Thomas, **56**
        White, John, **55**
    tankard
        Francis, Benjamin (poss.), **2**
    wine cooler
        Garrard I, Robert, **99**
cylinder
    apple corer, **65**
    beakers
        Harrison I, William or Hall I, William (poss.), **3**
    casters, 17
        Bellassye, William, **30**
    condiment pots
        Cripps, William (prob.), **84**
    inkstand pots
        Craig, John, **85**
    saucepans
        Crespell I, Sebastian & Crespell James, **88**
        Workman, Edward, **86**
ellipse
    cake basket
        Crespin, Paul, **67**
    dishes, meat
        Chawner, Henry, **92**
    ladles (in elevation)
        Storr, Paul, **94**
    nutmeg grater with corkscrew
        Parker, William, **97**
    salver (arcs of)
        Pero, John, **36**
    sauce-boats
        Tanqueray, Anne, **68**
    serving trowel
        Godfrey, Elizabeth, **75**
    spoon tray
        Payne, Humphrey, **19**
    sugar box with cover, **61**
    sweetmeat basket
        Parker I, John, & Wakelin, Edward, **81**
    toast-rack
        Roberts, Jr., Samuel, George Cadman and Co., **101**
    wine-bottle stand
        Gamon, John, **69**
ellipsoid
    ladles
        Storr, Paul, **94**
Lamé curves
    superellipse (?)
        tray
            Nelme, Anthony, **46**

Lamé curves *cont'd*
    subellipse (?)
        serving trowel
            Godfrey, Elizabeth, **75**
octofoil, 3, 4
    salver
        Pero, John, **36**
polygons
    dodecagon
        salver
            Mason, Thomas, **21**
    hexagon
        tapersticks
            Bird, Joseph, **27**
        teapot
            Pantin I, Simon, **50**
    octagon
        candlesticks
            Parr I, Thomas, **35**
        casters
            Chartier, John, **33**
            Jones, George Greenhill, **31**
            Jones I, John, **32**
        coffee pot
            Edwards II, John, **53**
        coral, 9
        cream jug
            Vincent, Edward, **16**,
        jugs
            hot-milk
                Batty II, Francis, **20**
        rattle and teether, **9**
        spoon
            Koop, Johannes, **24**
        strainer
            Gillingham, George, **34**
        sugar bowls
            Lofthouse, Seth, **15**
            Sanders I, John, **37**
                (with cover)
        teapot
            Dicken, Arthur, **44**
    quindecagon
        salver
            Courtauld, Augustine, *16*
pyramid
    coffee pot
        Edwards II, John, **53**
rectangle
    inkstand
        Craig, John, **85**
rectangle with canted corners
    salts, trencher
        Bolton, Thomas, **13**
    sugar boxes
        Chartier, John, **28**

rectangle with incurved
    corners
    salvers
        Feline, Edward, **72**
rectangle with rounded
    corners
    toasted-cheese dish
        McKay, John, Mackie,
            James, or McKenzie,
            James, **103**
    tray
        Payne, Humphrey, **22**
square with canted corners
    candlesticks
        Barnard I, John, **14**
geometry
    in metalwork in the Middle
        East and East Asia, 9, 19
    balusters in silver design, 17;
        ellipses in silver design,
        14–15; polygons in silver
        design, 14
Gillingham, George
    strainer, **34**
ginger-jars, Chinese
    design influence of, 17
goblets, 4, 5, 6
Godfrey, Benjamin, 89
Godfrey, Elizabeth
    serving trowel, **75**
Greene, Henry
    spoon, **25**
Gribelin, Simon, 50

Hall I, William (poss.)
    beaker, **3**
Hampden, John, 90
Hampston, John, & Prince, John
    saucepan, **89**
Harrison I, William (poss.)
    beaker, **3**
Harvey I, John
    wine syphon, **74**
Hase, Edward, 106
Havelaar, Adrian
    salver, **47**
Hennell, James Barclay
    cruet set, **107**
Hennell, Samuel
    candlestick, adjustable, **100**
heraldry
    arms (unascribed)
        chevron between three
            leopards' heads, **56**
        quarterly, 1 and 4, a tree
            and 2 and 3, a chevron
            between three martlets,
            3
    arms of
        Addington impaling those
            of another, **58**

arms of *cont'd*
    Alexander, with those of
        Euen on an escutcheon
        of pretence, **99**
    Armine family (lady of the),
        35
    Ashburnham, **54**
    Aston impaling those of
        another, **28**
    Bagot, **37**
    Bertie, Peregrine, 2nd Duke
        of Ancaster, **49**
    Bridgeman quartering
        Cradock with Mathews
        on an escutcheon of
        pretence, **22**
    Bullen impaling those of
        Aston, **68**
    Carr or Whiteman impaling
        those of Darcy or
        Sepham, **46**
    Duff impaling those of
        Grant, **36**
    Edgar quartering those of
        Sparrow, **39**
    England impaling those of
        Scotland, **53**
    Fountayne impaling those
        of Bromley, **67**
    France, **53**
    Gordon quartering those of
        probably Preston, **59**
    Gray impaling those of
        Chetwynd, **15**
    Hampden, John, **77**
    Hanover, **53**
    Hase, with those of Repps
        on an escutcheon of
        pretence, **93**
    Hutchinson, **66**
    Ireland, **53**
    King impaling those of Seys,
        55
    Meynell quartering those
        of Poyntz and Littleton
        and impaling those of
        Boothby quartering
        those of Scrymshire,
        82
    Mildmay quartering those
        of Fitzwalter with
        those of Schomberg
        on an escutcheon of
        pretence, **73**
    Montagu quarterly with
        those of Monthermer,
        21
    Pelham, **60**
    Petty quartering those of
        FitzMaurice, **50**
    Ramsay, **103**

arms of *cont'd*
    Stuart, John, 4th Earl of
        Bute, **92**
    Twysden impaling those of
        Finch, **1**
    Ward with many
        quarterings, **102**
    Watson, **44**
    Willem IV, **47**
badge of
    Pelham family, **38**
crest and coronet of
    Bass, Michael, 1st Baron
        Burton, **60**
    Curzon, Richard, 1st Earl
        Howe, **98**
    Fitzgerald, James, 20th Earl
        of Kildare, **78**
    Howe, Richard, 4th
        Viscount Howe, **84**
    Montagu, George, 1st Duke
        of Montagu, **88**
    Thynne, Thomas, 1st
        Marquess of Bath, **91**
crest of
    Ashley, **75**
    Crome, **40**
    Edgcumbe, **7**
    Newcomen family (prob.),
        79
crests (unascribed)
    cock, **90**
    martlet flanked by two
        plumes, **27**
    stag's head, **61**
    wyvern's head, **17**
monogram and coronet of
    Earl of Essex, **100**
Hogarth, William
    The Analysis of Beauty, 17, 17
honey skep
    Emes, Rebecca, & Barnard I,
        Edward, **98**
Honnecourt, Villard de, 10
Hougham, Solomon
    cheese stand, **95**
Howe, 1st Earl. *See* Curzon,
    Richard, 1st Earl Howe
Hunt, John Samuel
    stirrup cups, **104**, **106**

inkstand
    Craig, John, **85**
Irish silver
    caster, **17**
    kitchen pepper, **17**
    ladle, sauce (poss. Irish), **76**
    Barry, William (poss.)
        jug, hot-milk, **48**
    Bolton, Thomas
        salts, trencher, **13**

Craig, John
    inkstand, **85**
Nicholson, William (prob.)
    sugar bowl and cover, **52**
Rotheram, Caleb
    chocolate pot, **59**
Wilme I, John (prob.)
    egg frame, **79**
Workman, Edward
    saucepan, **86**

Jamnitzer, Wenzel
    *Perspectiva Corporum
    regularium*, 12
Jernegan, Henry, 95
Jewel Office, 42, 50, 51, 70, 88,
    91, 104
Jones I, John
    caster or kitchen pepper, **32**
Jones, George Greenhill
    caster or kitchen pepper, **31**
    saucepan, **18**
jugs. *See also* beer jug, cream
    jugs, *and* cow creamer
    hot-milk
        Barry, William (poss.), **48**
        Batty II, Francis, **20**

Kakiemon porcelain, 19
Kandler, Charles, 95, 96
Kandler, Charles Frederick, 96
Kandler, Frederick
    dishes, fluted, and covers, **82**
    verrières, 95, 96
Kändler, Johann Joachim, 96
Kepler, Johann
    Ad Vitellionem Paralipomena,
    14
Kildare, 20th Earl of. *See*
    Fitzgerald, James
King, 1st Baron. *See* King, Peter
King, Peter, 1st Baron King of
    Ockham, 73
kitchen peppers, 17
    Jones I, John, **32**
    Jones, George Greenhill, **31**
Koop, Johannes
    spoon with marrow spoon, **24**

ladles
    Mathew, William, **42**
    Storr, Paul, **94**
    sauce, **76**
Lamerie group, 81
Lamerie, Paul de, 74, 81, 88, 89,
    94
    dish, **73**
Leinster, 1st Duke of. *See*
    Fitzgerald, James
Lofthouse, Seth
    sugar bowl, **15**

Geometry and the Silversmith

London Patent Office, 116
lost-wax casting, 34

makers' marks (ascribed)
   BF, three pellets above, trefoil and two pellets below, in shield-shaped punch (Benjamin Francis, poss.), 2
   IR, crown above quatrefoil below (John Ruslen, prob.), 8
   SD, pellet below (Samuel Dell, poss.), 11
   WH, mullet above, pellet in annulet below (poss. either William Harrison I or William Hall I), 3
makers' marks (unascribed)
   cock on reversed C (?), 5
   IC, 76
   PD, three pellets above, cinquefoil below, 4
   RG, two hexafoils above, one below, 10
   RS above a heart and two pellets, 1
   TK, fleur-de-lis below, in shield-shaped punch, 7
   WC, mullet below, in shaped punch, 6
   WI in script, 9
marrow scoops or spoons. *See* spoons, marrow *and* spoons with marrow spoons
Mason, Thomas
   salver, 21
Mathew, William
   ladle, 42
Meale, George
   flask, 39
Methuen, George
   spice boxes, 77
Meynell, Hugo, 95–96, *96*
Meynell, Littleton Poyntz, 95
Mildmay, Benjamin, 1st Earl Fitzwalter, 85; inventory of his plate, *87*
mugs, 10
   Nelme, Francis, 58
mustard, 50, 98
mustard pot
   Hennell, James Barclay, 107

Nelme, Anthony
   salver, 46
Nelme, Francis
   mugs, 58
Newcastle, silver assayed in
   Batty II, Francis
      jug, hot-milk, 20
   Partis I, Thomas
      bowl, two-handled, 54
Newcastle-upon-Tyne, 1st Duke of. *See* Pelham-Holles, Thomas
Newenham, William, 69
Nicholson, William
   sugar bowl and cover (prob.), 52
Noy, Simon, 52
nutmeg grater with corkscrew
   Parker, William, 97

pail
   Wakelin, John, & Garrard I, Robert, 93
Pantin I, Simon, 89
   funnel, 70
   teapot, 50
Parker I, John, & Wakelin, Edward, 108
   sweetmeat basket, 81
Parker, William
   nutmeg grater with corkscrew, 97
Parr I, Thomas
   candlesticks, 35
Partis I, Thomas
   bowl, two-handled, 54
Payne, Humphrey
   spoon tray, 19
   tray, 22
Pelham-Holles, Thomas, 1st Duke of Newcastle-upon-Tyne, 57, 77, *77*
pepper, 37, 50
pepper boxes, 90
Pero, John
   salver, 36
Phillips, Humphrey (prob.)
   sugar tongs, 63
Platel, Pierre
   spoon, marrow, 66
plates, dinner
   Garthorne, Francis, 12
   Ruslen, John (prob.), 8
Pocock, Edward
   beakers, 71
Prince, John, & Hampston, John
   saucepan, 89
printed design sources
   Gribelin, Simon, 50
Pritchard, Thomas, 70
proportion and harmony, 17–18
provenance
   Bass, Michael, 1st Baron Burton, 60
   Bauer, Peter, Lord Bauer, 43
   Bertie, Peregrine, 2nd Duke of Ancaster, 49
   Bridgeman, Orlando, 5th Earl of Bradford, 22
   Bridgeman, Sir John, 22
   Browne, Denis, 10th Marquess of Sligo, 84
   Capel-Coningsby, George, 5th Earl of Essex, 100
   Capel, Adela, Countess of Essex, 100
   Chancellor, Sir Christopher, 36
   Cooper, H.A., 34
   Curzon, Richard, 1st Earl Howe, 98
   Duff, Arthur, 36
   Duff, William, 1st Earl Fife, 36
   Edgcumbe, Kenelm, 6th Earl of Mount Edgcumbe, 7
   Edgcumbe, Sir Richard (prob.), 7
   Egerton, Seymour, 6th Earl of Wilton, 2
   Esprito Santo Silva, Ricardo, 45
   Exeter College, Oxford, 96
   Fitzgerald, Edward, 7th Duke of Leinster, 78
   Fitzgerald, James, 20th Earl of Kildare, 78
   Fountayne, John, Dean of York, 67
   Fowler III, Francis E., 73
   Hahn family, 42
   Hamilton, Angus, 15th Duke of Hamilton and 12th Duke of Brandon, 94
   Hamilton, Archibald, 9th Duke of Hamilton and 6th Duke of Brandon, 94
   Hampden, John, 77
   Hamwee, Neville, 60
   Hase, Edward, 93
   How of Edinburgh Ltd., 45
   Howe, Louisa Catherine, 84
   Howe, Richard, 4th Viscount Howe, 84
   Hue-Williams, Mrs Vera, 2
   James Walker Collection of Silver and Vertu, 88, 105
   King, Manon, Countess of Lovelace, 55
   King, Peter, 1st Baron King, 55
   Lockett, George A., 2
   Lumley, Thomas, 82
   Mackay, Hon. A.J.F., 1
   Mallaby-Deeley, Sir Harry, 78
   Meynell, Hugo, 82
   Mildmay, Benjamin, 1st Earl Fitzwalter, 73
   Montagu, George, 1st Duke of Montagu, 88
   Palladio Stiftung (Liechtenstein), 44, 68
   Pelham-Holles, Thomas, 1st Duke of Newcastle-upon-Tyne, 38, 60
   Petterson, R.L., 54
   Petty-FitzMaurice, Edmond, 1st Baron FitzMaurice, 50
   Plohn, Mrs Fay, 36
   Raphael, Ernest, 17
   Reif, Consul F.C., 5
   Reksten, Hilmar, 36
   Rochdale, St John, 2nd Viscount Rochdale, 59
   Rothschild, Nathaniel, 3rd Baron Rothschild, 7, 84
   Stuart, John, 4th Earl of Bute, 92
   Thynne, Alexander, 7th Marquess of Bath, 91
   Thynne, Thomas, 1st Marquess of Bath, 91
   Tod, Anne Helen, 36
   Trustees of the Longleat Chattels Settlement, 91
   Twysden, Anne, Lady Twysden, 1
   Vierssen, Jonkheer J.W. van, 47
   Ward, John, 1st Earl of Dudley, 102
   Wharton, Jemima, 36
   Wharton, Richard, 36
   Willson, Walter H., 45
Punch, Judy and Toby cruet set
   Hennell, James Barclay, 107
punch-bowl, 72
Pyne, Benjamin
   sugar bowl and cover, 51

Queen Anne taste, 18–19, 21

rattle and teether, 9
Robert Hennell and Sons
   cruet set, 107
   stirrup cup, 105
Roe, Nathaniel
   spoon with marrow spoon, 23
Roestraeten, Pieter van, 20
Rollos, John, 42
Rotheram, Caleb
   chocolate pot, 59
Rundell, Bridge and Rundell, 107, 110, 115, 116
Ruslen, John
   plate (prob.), 8

Sadler, Thomas
   spoon, 26

The Domcha Collection

salts, trencher, **7**
   Bolton, Thomas, **13**
salvers
   Courtauld, Augustine, *16*
   Feline, Edward, **72**
   Havelaar, Adrian, **47**
   Mason, Thomas, **21**
   Nelme, Anthony, **46**
   Pero, John, **36**
sand-casting, 34
Sanders I, John
   sugar bowl and cover, **37**
sauce-boats
   Tanqueray, Anne, **68**
saucepans
   Crespell I, Sebastian, &
     Crespell James, **88** (with cover)
   Hampston, John, & Prince, John, **89**
   Jones, George Greenhill, **18**
   Wastell, Samuel, **29**
   Wakelin, John, & Tayler, William, **90** (with cover)
   Workman, Edward, **86**
saucers, 57
Scarlett, William, 44
Schuppe, John
   cow creamer, **80**
scoops, marrow. *See* spoons, marrow *and* spoons with marrow spoons
Scottish silversmiths
   Mackie, James, **114**
   McKay, John (prob.)
     dish, toasted-cheese, **103**
   McKenzie, James, **114**
Seabrook, James, 50
service à la française, 33, 44, 88
serving trowel
   Godfrey, Elizabeth, **75**
shapes, general. *See also* geometrical shapes
   baluster
     beer jug
       Farren, Thomas, **45**
     candlesticks
       Parr I, Thomas, **35**
     casters
       Chartier, John, **33**
       Jones I, John, **32**
     coral, **9**
     cream jug
       Wastell, Samuel. **62**
       Vincent, Edward, **16**
     goblets, **4**, **5**, **6**
     jugs, hot-milk
       Barry, William, **48**
       Batty II, Francis, **20**
     mugs
       Nelme, Francis, **58**

shapes, general, baluster *cont'd*
     rattle and teether, **9**
     saucepan
       Wastell, Samuel, **29**
     tapersticks
       Bird, Joseph, **27**
   globe
     teapots
       Dicken, Arthur, **44**
       Pantin I, Simon, **50**
   oblong
     dishes, fluted (octangular)
       Kandler, Frederick, **82**
     flask
       Meale, George, **39**
     tray
       Nelme, Anthony, **46**
   radiating fluting
     dishes
       Kandler, Frederick, **82**
       Willaume I, David, **38**
       Willaume II, David, **60**
   spoon tray
     Payne, Humphrey, **19**
Sheffield silversmiths
   Samuel Roberts, Jr, George Cadman and Co.
     toast rack, **101**
shop signs
   Bell (Skinner Row, Dublin), 66
   Golden Cup, 31
   Golden Ring, 39
   Hen and Chickens, 38
   Mitre, 95
   Sun, 95
Sleath, Gabriel, 74
Smith, John, 59
spice boxes
   Methuen, George, **77**
spoon tray
   Payne, Humphrey, **19**
spoons
   Greene, Henry, **25**
   Sadler, Thomas, **26**
   basting, 44
   marrow
     Koop, Johannes, **24**
     Platel, Pierre, **66**
     Roe, Nathaniel, **23**
   serving, and fork
     Bateman, Peter & Ann, **96**
   strainer
     Archer, Andrew, **41**
     Looker, William, **43**
   with marrow spoons
     Koop, Johannes, **24**
     Roe, Nathaniel, **23**
Stackhouse, Thomas
   sugar tongs, **64**

stirrup cups
   Hennell, James Barclay, **105**
   Hunt, John Samuel, **104**, **106**
   Storr, Paul, 115
     ladles, **94**
strainer
   Gillingham, George, **34**
   Stuart, John, 4th Earl of Bute, 104
sugar bowls
   Lofthouse, Seth, **15**
   with covers, **61**
     Nicholson, William (prob.), 52
     Pyne, Benjamin, **51**
     Sanders I, John, **37**
sugar boxes
   Chartier, John, **28**
   with cover, **61**
sugar tongs
   Phillips, Humphrey (prob.), **63**
   Stackhouse, Thomas, **64**
sweetmeat basket
   Parker I, John, & Wakelin, Edward, **81**

tankard
   Francis, Benjamin (poss.), **2**
   Tanqueray, Anne
     sauce-boats, **68**
tapersticks
   Bird, Joseph, **27**
Tayler, William, & Wakelin, John
   casserole and cover, **91**
   saucepan and cover, **90**
teapots
   Dicken, Arthur, **44**
   Fawdery, William, **49**
   Pantin I, Simon, **50**
Tearle, Thomas
   coffee pot, **56**
teether and rattle, **9**
Thynne, Thomas, 1st Marquess of Bath, 103
toast-rack
   Samuel Roberts, Jr, George Cadman and Co., **101**
trays
   Payne, Humphrey, **22**
   Garrard II, Robert, **102** (knife or pipe)
tumbler cups, 91
   Dell, Samuel (poss.), **11**
Twysden, Anne, Lady Twysden, 25
Twysden, Sir William, 25

Uccello, Paolo, 12, *12*

verrières
   Kandler, Frederick, 95, *96*

Vincent, Edward
   cream jug, **16**
Vitruvius
   De Architectura, 18; (detail from French edition), *18*

waiter
   Cooper I, Matthew, **57**
Wakelin, Edward, & Parker I, John, 108
   sweetmeat basket, **81**
Wakelin, John, & Garrard I, Robert
   pail, **93**
Wakelin, John, & Tayler, William
   casserole and cover, **91**
   saucepan and cover, **90**
Ward, John, 1st Earl of Dudley, 113
Wastell, Samuel
   cream jug, **62**
   saucepan, **29**
Weymouth, Thomas, 3rd Viscount of. *See* Thynne, Thomas, 1st Marquess of Bath
White, John
   coffee pot, **55**
Wickes, George, 94, 102
   beakers, nesting, **78**
   coffee pot, 14, *15*
wig duster
   Bellassye, William, **30**
Wilks, James (prob.)
   flask, **40**
Willaume I, David, 76, 82
   dishes, fluted, **38**
Willaume II, David
   dishes, fluted, **60**
Williamson, John, 92
Wilme I, John (prob.)
   egg frame, **79**
wine cooler
   Garrard I, Robert, **99**
wine pot, Chinese, 20, *20*
wine siphon
   Harvey I, John, **74**
wine-bottle stand
   Gamon, John, **69**
Wisdome, John, 85
Workman, Edward
   saucepan, **86**

York, silver assayed in
   Hampston, John, & Price, John
     saucepan, **89**